ENCYCLOPEDIA of INSECTS

WIDE EYED EDITIONS

CONTENTS

4-5	INTRODUCTION FROM THE AUTHOR	40-51	HEMIPTERA (WATER BUGS, CICADAS, FROGHOPPERS, TREEHOPPERS, ASSASSIN BUGS, SHIELD BUGS, JEWEL BUGS, APHIDS, MOSS BUGS, AND SCALE INSECTS)
6-7	INSECTS IN TROUBLE		
8-9	WHAT IS AN INSECT?		
10-11	INSECT FEATS		
12-13	EPHEMEROPTERA (MAYFLIES)	52-68	HYMENOPTERA (BEES, WASPS, SAWFLIES, AND ANTS)
14-17	ODONATA (DRAGONFLIES AND DAMSELFLIES)	69	STREPSIPTERA (TWISTED-WINGED INSECTS)
18-23	ORTHOPTERA (GRASSHOPPERS, LOCUSTS, AND CRICKETS)	70-97	COLEOPTERA (BEETLES)
		98-99	MEGALOPTERA (DOBSONFLIES, FISHFLIES AND ALDERFLIES)
24-25	PHASMATODEA (STICK INSECTS)	100-101	TRICHOPTERA (CADDISFLIES)
26-27	PLECOPTERA (STONEFLIES)	102-119	LEPIDOPTERA (MOTHS AND BUTTERFLIES)
28-29	DERMAPTERA (EARWIGS)	120-135	DIPTERA (FLIES)
30-31	MANTODEA (MANTISES)	136-137	ARCHAEOGNATHA (JUMPING BRISTLETAILS) AND ZYGENTOMA (FIREBRATS AND SILVERFISH)
32-33	BLATTODEA (COCKROACHES AND TERMITES)		
34-35	PSOCOPTERA (BOOKLICE)	138-139	NEUROPTERA (NET-WINGED INSECTS) AND RAPHIDIOPTERA (SNAKEFLIES)
36-37	PHTHIRAPTERA (LICE)		
38-39	THYSANOPTERA (THRIPS)	140-141	MECOPTERA (SCORPIONFLIES) AND NOTOPTERA (GLADIATORS)

142-143	**ZORAPTERA (ANGEL INSECTS) AND EMBIOPTERA (WEBSPINNERS)**
144-145	**SIPHONAPTERA (FLEAS)**
146-157	**AM I AN INSECT?**
148-149	**CENTIPEDES AND MILLIPEDES**
150-151	**SPIDERS AND SPIDERLIKE INVERTEBRATES**
152-153	**WOODLICE**
154-155	**SNAILS AND SLUGS**
156-159	**INDEX**

HOW TO USE THIS BOOK

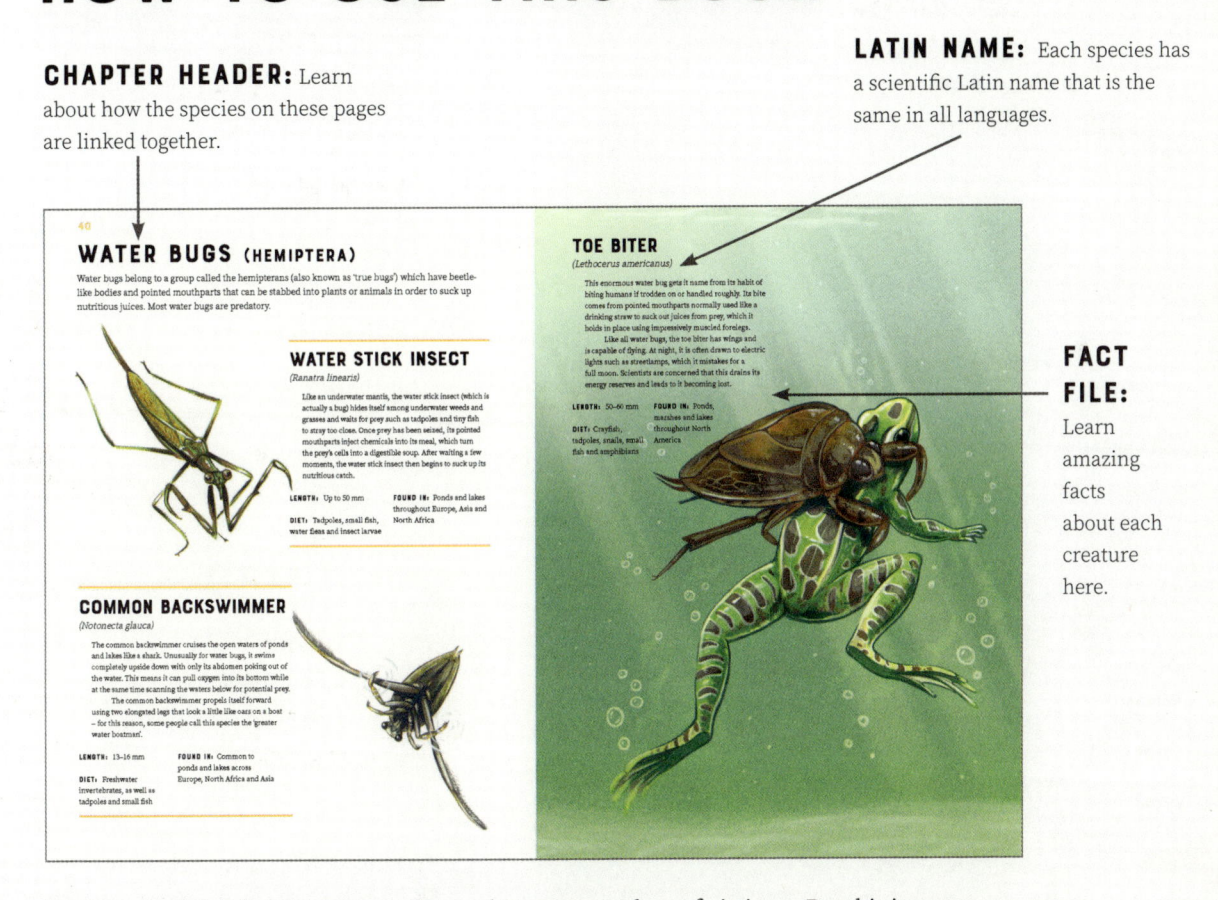

CHAPTER HEADER: Learn about how the species on these pages are linked together.

LATIN NAME: Each species has a scientific Latin name that is the same in all languages.

FACT FILE: Learn amazing facts about each creature here.

WATER BUGS (HEMIPTERA)

Water bugs belong to a group called the hemipterans (also known as 'true bugs') which have beetle-like bodies and pointed mouthparts that can be stabbed into plants or animals in order to suck up nutritious juices. Most water bugs are predatory.

WATER STICK INSECT
(Ranatra linearis)

Like an underwater mantis, the water stick insect (which is actually a bug) hides itself among underwater weeds and grasses and waits for prey such as tadpoles and tiny fish to stray too close. Once prey has been seized, its pointed mouthparts inject chemicals into its meal, which turn the prey's cells into a digestible soup. After waiting a few moments, the water stick insect then begins to suck up its nutritious catch.

LENGTH: Up to 50 mm
DIET: Tadpoles, small fish, water fleas and insect larvae
FOUND IN: Ponds and lakes throughout Europe, Asia and North Africa

COMMON BACKSWIMMER
(Notonecta glauca)

The common backswimmer cruises the open waters of ponds and lakes like a shark. Unusually for water bugs, it swims completely upside down with only its abdomen poking out of the water. This means it can pull oxygen into its bottom while at the same time scanning the waters below for potential prey.
The common backswimmer propels itself forward using two elongated legs that look a little like oars on a boat – for this reason, some people call this species the 'greater water boatman'.

LENGTH: 13-16 mm
DIET: Freshwater invertebrates, as well as tadpoles and small fish
FOUND IN: Common to ponds and lakes across Europe, North Africa and Asia

TOE BITER
(Lethocerus americanus)

This enormous water bug gets its name from its habit of biting humans if trodden on or handled roughly. Its bite comes from pointed mouthparts normally used like a drinking straw to suck out juices from prey, which it holds in place using impressively muscled foreregs.
Like all water bugs, the toe biter has wings and is capable of flying. At night, it is often drawn to electric lights such as streetlamps, which it mistakes for a full moon. Scientists are concerned that this drains its energy reserves and leads to it becoming lost.

LENGTH: 50-60 mm
DIET: Crayfish, tadpoles, snails, small fish and amphibians
FOUND IN: Ponds, marshes and lakes throughout North America

You can read this book in any order and in any number of sittings. Read it in your seat, or take it out into the wild. Read about the creatures you know you love, and then discover many more you had no idea existed!

INTRODUCTION FROM THE AUTHOR

IF ALIENS WERE TO VISIT OUR PLANET AND MAKE A LIST OF ALL OF EARTH'S ANIMALS, THEY WOULD QUICKLY SEE A PATTERN.

Nearly every single one of this planet's creatures, they would notice, are from one strange group that has six legs, three segments to their body, and, often, a pair of wings. We call these organisms the insects. Because the insect group accounts for 90% of life forms on this planet, alien visitors would be correct in calling this the Planet of Insects. Truly, this is an insect world. You and I just happen to live on it.

The scale of insect life on Earth really is astounding. Insects far outnumber people, and then some. For every single human, there are literally trillions of insects of millions of different species, many not yet named by scientists. They live in our houses, on our trees, in the soil, on the highest mountains, and in the deepest rivers. In the billions, insects buzz, weave, and scramble through rainforests and woodlands. They thrive in grasslands, deserts, and wastelands. They paralyze, they pollinate, they prance, and they prowl.

In addition to this, there is not a food source on Earth that comes close to that provided by insects—most birds, reptiles, and many mammals could not live without the food that they supply. In fact, insects help us in all sorts of ways.

Take the lowly bee, for instance. Overall, there are more than 5,000 species of bee on Earth and each day thousands of millions of them move busily from flower to flower in search of nectar. In return for this sugary fluid, the bees carry the flower's pollen around, helping plants to reproduce and stay healthy in their war against plant diseases. As much as 10% of food produced by farmers arrives on our plates because of insect pollinators like bees working hard on our behalf. That means that one in every ten mouthfuls of food you've swallowed in your life has been because of insects.

There are other ways that insects help humans. Without silkmoth caterpillars, for instance, there would be no silk. Without flesh-eating beetles and flies, the dead bodies of frogs, birds, and foxes would litter the landscape. Without crunchy crickets to eat, one thousand million humans would go hungry. And lastly, and perhaps most shocking of all, without pollinating midges there would be no chocolate!

However, although they are numerous and diverse, the insects are not invincible. Over the last 30 years, scientists from all around the world have noticed that there are many fewer insects around than there once were.

Many insect species are facing extinction because their precious habitats are being destroyed or because the air that they breathe is being polluted. Our changing climate is also causing some insects to disappear. The powerful weather events that climate change brings, for instance, mean that the fate of almost every insect species is more uncertain than it ever has been.

And so, if I have one aim in writing this book, it is this: to share my love of insects with you, the reader, so that you can get a feel for this awe-inspiring group of animals and commit to helping them survive for as long as possible. After all, we cannot save what we do not know.

Together with beautiful painted illustrations provided by Miranda Zimmerman, we want to inspire you to look out for and study these unsung heroes of the natural world. To come to know them. To know their names. To shout from the rooftops about how amazing they are. And, hopefully, to give a helping hand in bringing them back to a former glory.

This really is the Planet of the Insects, after all. I hope, through books like this one, that we can keep it that way.

INSECTS IN TROUBLE

Insects are tremendously tough. As a group, insects have survived the meteorite that killed off most of the dinosaurs, and the intense droughts and floods that occurred for millions of years before. They have survived ice ages and earthquakes, and the most epic storms ever known. Yet, in the modern day, insects face a new threat—humans.

In recent times, humans are changing the planet in lots of different ways all at once. At this exact moment, for instance, tropical forests are being cut down or burned to make space for cattle farming. Wetlands are being drained to make places to plant crops. Hedgerows and meadows are being removed to make space for new houses or roads. But these places provide important homes for thousands of different kinds of insects. When these habitats disappear, so too do the insects that have adapted to live there. Often, they are gone forever.

Scientists from around the world have only recently started looking at how many insects may be suffering from widespread changes to habitats that humans are causing. What these scientists are discovering is very worrying. Almost half of the 180,000 known species of moths and butterflies are likely to be drifting slowly toward extinction, and many beetles, for example, are close behind. Pollinating insects, including many species of bee and fly, are also edging closer and closer to disappearing forever.

The fact that Earth's climate is changing causes more problems for some insects. Long weeks of unpredictable winter storms, for instance, can kill off food plants for insect larvae, squeezing some unique insect species closer and closer toward extinction. Likewise, climate change can cause long periods of warmer weather, which allows more competitive insect species to move in, pushing native insects out of the ecosystem jobs they need to survive. These ecosystem invaders can also bring with them diseases, some of which can be dangerous to humans.

More than any other group of animals on Earth, the insects are true survivors. For this reason, it is highly unlikely that our changing planet will lead to the loss of every insect species. However, it is clear that the survival of some of the most charismatic and beneficial insect species is far from secure and so we must do all we can to save them.

WHAT CAN YOU DO TO HELP INSECTS?

1. GET TO KNOW INSECTS

To love something, you first of all have to spend some time with it. Soak up as much as you can about insects, using books like this one or by studying those insects closest to you, in your garden or school playground. If you don't know what insect species you are looking at, then sketch an illustration or take a photo and send it to a local museum. Often, they will be delighted to help you work out what sort of insect it is.

2. MAKE YOUR NEIGHBORHOOD INSECT-FRIENDLY

Insects love places to feed, places to hide, and places to lay their eggs. You can encourage insects into your garden or local area by planting lots of wildflowers where pollinating insects can gather nectar and by adding woodpiles in which they can seek shelter. If you have a grass lawn, consider letting some areas grow long to provide places for insects to hide and keep cool in the summer sun.

3. TAKE PART IN CITIZEN SCIENCE!

Many of the facts in this book have been gathered by amateur insect-lovers working together to discover new things. For instance, to help understand how far the painted lady butterfly (see page 115) migrates, teams of people across Europe kept a lookout for them and reported when and where they saw them flying. This so-called citizen science is likely to become very important in helping scientists discover new things about insects. Your school or local museum might be able to tell you of citizen science schemes that you can join.

WHAT IS AN INSECT?

Insects can be told apart from other armored invertebrates such as spiders and crabs by looking for the key features you can see on this page.

THREE-PART BODY

Long before the dinosaurs, insects hit upon a body pattern that allowed them to be flexible, yet tough. Insect bodies are divided into three parts—a head, thorax, and abdomen. The head is covered in sensory apparatus, which helps the insect find what it needs; the thorax is where all of the digestive organs are found; and the abdomen is where the organs responsible for reproduction are found. The abdomen also contains little holes along the sides called spiracles, which are like mini-lungs and used to pull oxygen into the body. This three-part body plan holds true for all insects, though in some insects, such as beetles and true bugs, the thorax is harder to see.

SIX JOINTED LEGS

All insects have three pairs of legs which protrude (stick out) from the thorax of the insect. In most species, the legs are primarily used for walking, but in many species, such as mantises and water stick insects, the forelegs are adapted into clawed appendages used for attacking prey.

EYES

Nearly all insects have a pair of compound eyes. Compound eyes differ from our own eyes because they are made up of thousands of tiny lenses which pick up lots of images at once. Compound eyes help insects spot movement from many angles at once—this gives insects superfast reflexes.

Many insects also have a number of smaller eyespots on the top of the head (called ocelli). Ocelli are very sensitive to spotting the shadows of approaching predators, such as birds. They are especially easy to see in wasps.

WINGS

Many insects have wings, either double-paired (in the case of butterflies and moths) or single-paired (in the case of flies). Many insects, including mayflies, ants, and many grasshoppers, only develop wings in the final stage of their life when seeking mates. Once she has mated, a queen ant will chew off her wings before getting on with the business of egg-laying.

LIFE-STAGES

COMPLETE METAMORPHOSIS

The vast majority of insects have a life cycle that begins with an egg, from which hatches a wormlike stage (called a larva), which seals itself into a chamber (a pupa) in which it changes into a final adult form. This is called "complete metamorphosis."

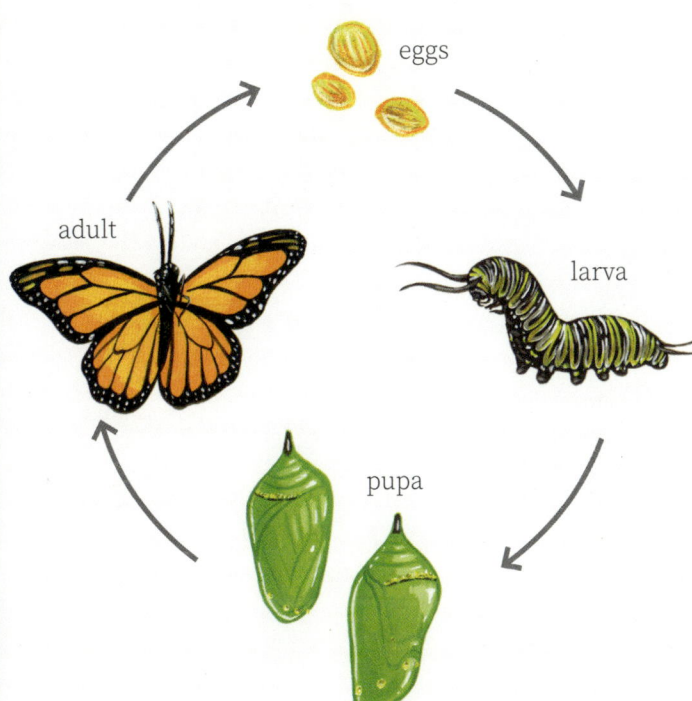

The wormlike larva can be called many things depending on the species. In butterflies, the larvae are called caterpillars. In beetles, they are called grubs. Maggots are the larvae of flies. Some beetles and lacewings have very active larvae with large mouthparts used for hunting. These are called "campodeiform" larvae.

Nearly all of the largest insect groups have a life cycle involving complete metamorphosis, including butterflies and moths, beetles and flies. The reason this life strategy is so successful for so many insects is probably because the larvae do not compete for the same food as the adults. This means there is more food to go around for everyone.

INCOMPLETE METAMORPHOSIS

Many insects, including the true bugs, dragonflies, cockroaches, grasshoppers and stick insects, hatch from eggs as miniature versions of their adult form. As these young insects grow, they periodically shed their skin in a process called molting. With each molt, young insects grow larger and larger. This is called "incomplete metamorphosis."

Young insects that molt in this way are called nymphs. In the final molt, many species take on a form capable of reproduction, often complete with wings that help them find potential mates.

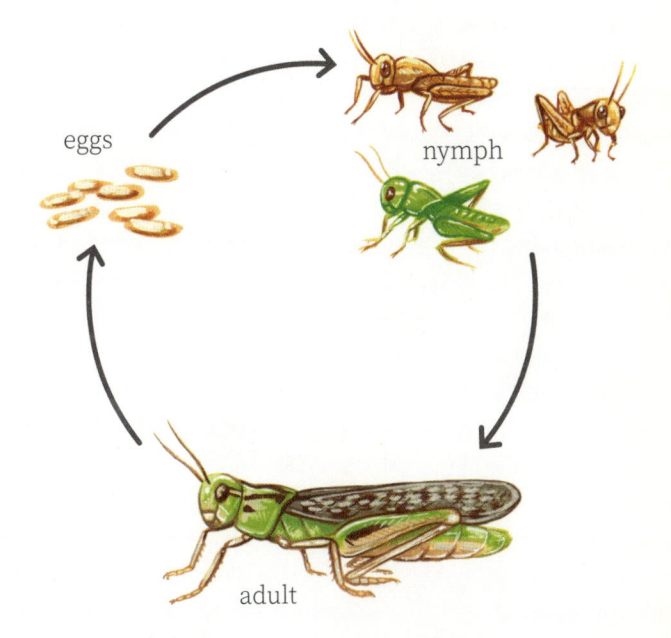

INSECT FEATS

UP HIGH
Each day as the sun rises, many millions of flying insects take to the skies to move from feeding place to feeding place or to find mates. Often, these insects drift on invisible winds high up in the atmosphere. Here they are followed by insect-hunters such as high-flying birds and dragonflies. For the highest altitude, the globe skimmer (see page 15) holds the record. This dragonfly has been spotted more than 20,000 feet above sea level.

DOWN LOW
Alongside scorpions and spiders, insects are well equipped to colonize the deepest and darkest of planet Earth's caves. Often these cave-dwelling insects have tiny eyes and move around following scent trails on the cave floor. Springtails are among the most common of cave insects, and have been discovered in caves that are more than half a mile below the surface of Earth.

SUPER SOUNDS
By scraping their body parts together or by passing air in and out of their bodies, many insects can make a range of sounds, including hissing, screeching, and chirping. For their size, insects make some of the loudest noises in the animal kingdom. One tiny water bug called *Micronecta scholtzi* can produce more than 99.2 decibels of noise—this is the equivalent to a full orchestra of instruments playing as loud as possible within a few feet of your ears. The male uses this extra-loud song in springtime to call for females.

OUT AT SEA
In the sea, the crustaceans are king. Because of this, insects have struggled to colonize the oceans. However, one group of species has managed to make the waves their own—the mysterious sea skaters. These insects are part of a group called the hemipterans (or 'true bugs'). They skate along the surface tension of the water searching for prey hidden a few inches beneath. As with many insects, scientists know little about them and are eager to learn more.

ECHOLOCATE

Where bats use sound waves to understand their surroundings, some insects use water waves. One group of water beetles (known as whirligig beetles) can send pressure waves across the surface of a pond or lake and then feel for reflections of these pressure waves as they bounce off nearby objects. Echolocating in this way helps whirligig beetles work out where potential rival beetles may be lurking.

GLOW IN THE DARK

By producing special chemicals, many insects can make their abdomens glow or flash with color. In the case of fireflies, this ghostly green light can be used to attract a mate on warm, dark nights. Some insect larvae can also wield light in this way. The wormlike larvae of one tiny fly species called *Arachnocampa luminosa* (see page 135) uses light to attract flies, which it catches in a drip of slime and later devours.

FAST LIVES

Being small and quick to grow, many insects live fast and die young. This is especially true of species that live near freshwater, such as stoneflies and mayflies. The aquatic nymphs of these species may live in water for two or three years, but as winged adults die within hours. The record holder for the shortest life span is a mayfly called *Dolania americana*. In its adult form, this species lays eggs and dies within five minutes.

CHEMICAL COMMUNICATION

When trying to find a mate, many insects produce special chemicals called pheromones. These pheromones are often used as scent trails that help insects meet one another for mating. In many species of butterfly and moth, for instance, pheromones can be detected from more than 6 miles away.

SUPER SWARMS

Some insects are known for their ability to swarm together in large groups, sometimes made up of a million or more individuals. Large swarms like these can protect insects from predators or help them find new food sources. Some locust species can swarm in vast clouds nearly 400 square miles in size. These swarms are filled with billions of locusts that eat everything in their path.

SPEED

Although many insects depend on wings to move from place to place, some species spend their lives sprinting across the ground in search of food and shelter. Among the world's fastest insects are the Australian tiger beetles, which can cover a distance of over 8 feet in a single second. For their size, that's almost 30 times faster than a human athlete running the Olympic 100-meter sprint.

MAYFLIES (EPHEMEROPTERA)

Mayflies first appeared in the world long before dinosaurs, more than 300 million years ago. Mayflies live most of their life underwater as nymphs. Some species live only a few days as flying adults, hence the word "ephemero" in their scientific name—"ephemeral" means "short-lived."

GREEN DRAKE MAYFLY
(Ephemera danica)

After a year or two spent underwater as a nymph, the adult green drake mayfly emerges from the water and takes to the sky. In a matter of days, the female will make lots of visits to rivers and streams, gently putting the tip of her tail under the water to squirt out eggs. In all, she lays 8,000 eggs before dying of exhaustion.

The green drake mayfly is one of Europe's most common mayfly species. It prefers clean, unpolluted rivers, lakes, and streams.

LENGTH: .6–.8 in.

FOUND IN: Rivers and lakes throughout Europe

DIET: Nymphs feed by filtering food particles from out of the water

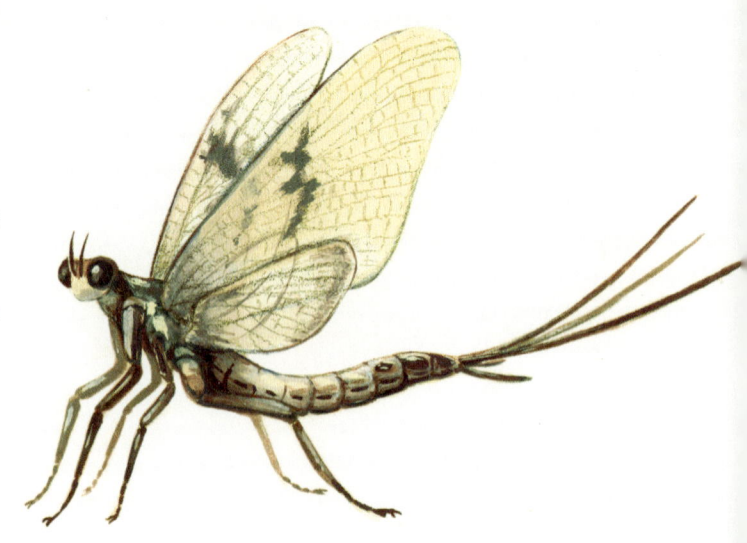

SEPIA DUN
(Leptophlebia marginata)

The sepia dun is a world-conquering mayfly. It lives throughout much of the Northern Hemisphere and is drawn to the edges of lakes and ponds where the water is still and clean.

Like other mayflies, nymphs of the sepia dun often emerge as adults from the water all at the same time. This can lead to spectacular clouds of adult mayflies, each thousands strong, exploding into the evening sky. These swarms are an important food source for predators such as bats and birds, which hoover them up hungrily.

LENGTH: .25–.4 in.

FOUND IN: Lakes and ponds throughout northern regions of North America, Europe, and Asia

DIET: Nymphs are filter-feeders

TISZA MAYFLY
(Palingenia longicauda)

This large mayfly is named after the Tisza river in Central Europe where it lives. A single square metre of mud from this river may be home to up to 400 burrowing nymphs. The nymphs live for a year in the water before emerging as adults in their millions. So spectacular is the mass-emergence of this mayfly that it has become an annual tourist attraction. Local people call it the 'blooming of the Tisza'.

Sadly, many parts of the Tisza river no longer contain this impressive mayfly because it is very sensitive to pollution.

LENGTH: 4.7 in.

DIET: Nymphs filter-feed tiny food particles from water

FOUND IN: The Tisza river of central and eastern Europe

STENACRON MAYFLY
(Stenacron interpunctatum)

Like all mayflies, the adult stenacron mayfly cannot eat. Its mouthparts are small and its digestive system is filled with nothing but air. Once it emerges, it must find a mate quickly before burning through its energy reserves and dying of exhaustion. To help them find a mate quickly, male mayflies of this species are armed with extra-large eyes for spotting females as they fly across the water surface.

Stenacron nymphs like to rest underneath stones in fast-flowing water. They are extra streamlined to help them cling on.

LENGTH: .4–.6 in.

DIET: Nymphs are filter-feeders of fast-moving streams

FOUND IN: Fast-flowing streams throughout Canada and the US

DRAGONFLIES (ODONATA)

Dragonflies are skilled aerial predators that fly upon powerful wings which allow them to hover in search of prey, before quickly giving chase. In all, 3,000 species live today. Dragonflies are associated with freshwater because their nymphs are aquatic.

SCARLET DWARF DRAGONFLY
(Nannophya pygmaea)

The scarlet dwarf dragonfly is the world's smallest dragonfly. While some dragonflies can have a wingspan of almost 6 in. or more, its total wingspan is just .78 in. across, meaning it could perch quite happily on the tip of your finger.

To tiny flies, the scarlet dwarf is an eagle-like predator, however. It waits beside lakes and ponds, searching for these miniscule insects as they hatch from the surface. When it spots a potential meal, it zooms over, lunging at its prey with its long legs outstretched.

WINGSPAN: .78 in.

DIET: Small flies and other invertebrates

FOUND IN: Throughout Southeast Asia, China, and Japan

COMMON GREEN DARNER
(Anax junius)

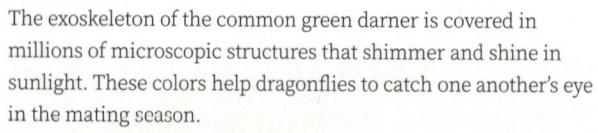

The exoskeleton of the common green darner is covered in millions of microscopic structures that shimmer and shine in sunlight. These colors help dragonflies to catch one another's eye in the mating season.

Dragonflies lay their eggs on pond plants, curving their abdomens into the water to attach them firmly. The aquatic nymphs that hatch from these eggs look a little bit like adult dragonflies except their bodies lack wings. Dragonfly nymphs terrorize other pond invertebrates, attacking them with jaws that snap out from their faces with lightning speed.

WINGSPAN: Up to 3.15 in.

DIET: Flying ants, moths, and flies

FOUND IN: Common throughout North America

EMPEROR DRAGONFLY
(Anax imperator)

The emperor dragonfly flies much higher than many other dragonflies. Like a bird of prey, it looks for telltale silhouettes of prey, including moths and butterflies, flying beetles, and even spiders blown off their webs.

The emperor dragonfly spots prey using eyes that can see in almost every direction at once. Each of its eyes is made up of almost 24,000 mini eyes that register the movement of objects nearby. These are called compound eyes. All insects have compound eyes, but the compound eyes of dragonflies are among the most well adapted.

WINGSPAN: Up to 4.3 in.

FOUND IN: Throughout Africa, Europe, and Asia

DIET: Medium-sized flying insects

GLOBE SKIMMER
(Pantala flavescens)

The globe skimmer is aptly named. Not only has it been seen on every continent except Antarctica, the species is also celebrated for being the farthest long-distance traveler of any insect. Some globe skimmers manage to travel more than 3,700 miles in a single lifetime. They occasionally turn up on desert islands, thousands of miles away from their natural freshwater surroundings.

Like soaring birds of prey, globe skimmers sometimes form large swarms above invisible currents of hot air that rise from rocks that have been warmed by the sun.

WINGSPAN: 2.8–3.3 in.

FOUND IN: Across most of the world

DIET: Mosquitoes, flying ants, and termites

DAMSELFLIES (ODONATA)

There are almost 3,000 species of damselfly on Earth and each is a dynamic aerial hunter of other invertebrates. Damselflies can be told apart from dragonflies because most damselflies rest their wings against their body when they land. Dragonflies, on the other hand, rest with their wings held outward like an airplane.

GIANT HELICOPTER DAMSELFLY

(Megaloprepus caerulatus)

The giant helicopter damselfly is a hunter of secretive web-spinning spiders, which it plucks from webs using spiky legs that act like claws. Its long wings provide for a powerful lift-off. The male uses the conspicuous bands of black color on its wings to grab the attention of nearby females.

The giant helicopter damselfly has the largest wingspan of any living dragonfly or damselfly species, but its size is nothing compared to those of its prehistoric relatives, some of whom had a wingspan of nearly 2.5 feet across.

WINGSPAN: Up to 7.5 in.　**FOUND IN:** Rainforests of Central and South America
DIET: Spiders

BEAUTIFUL DEMOISELLE

(Calopteryx virgo)

The beautiful demoiselle gets its name from its glittering green color and for its shimmering patterned wings. When a female passes through a male's territory, the male uses these decorated wings to try and catch her eye.

The male beautiful demoiselle is fiercely competitive. Should a male accidentally stray into another male's territory, both begin to flash their wings angrily at one another to show off their size and strength. If that doesn't scare one of the males off, aerial battles between them can sometimes break out.

WINGSPAN: 2.4–2.9 in.　**FOUND IN:** Near fast-flowing streams and rivers throughout Europe
DIET: Small flying insects

AZURE DAMSELFLY
(Coenagrion puella)

The azure damselfly rarely likes to fly out across the open waters of a lake or a pond. Instead it prefers the tangled leaves and grasses at the waters' edge. Like a stealthy helicopter it slowly moves through the undergrowth, using its large eyes to spot resting mosquitoes and other small flies on the undersides of plants. When it spots a potential meal, the azure damselfly lunges with its legs outstretched. After pulling its meal upward, it makes a cage out of its legs that stops its prey escaping.

WINGSPAN: 1.6 in.

FOUND IN: Ponds and lakes across many parts of Europe

DIET: Mosquitoes and other small flying insects

GRASSHOPPERS (ORTHOPTERA)

In all, approximately 11,000 grasshopper species are known today and nearly all species are capable of making giant leaps courtesy of their long back legs. In the early days of the dinosaurs, grasshoppers were one of the first insects to hit upon a plant-eating way of life.

RAINBOW GRASSHOPPER
(Dactylotum bicolor)

The rainbow grasshopper uses its vivid colors to warn lizards of its disgusting taste. Its strange patterns are different, depending on where exactly the species is found. Individuals from the US are a deeper red, for instance, while those from Mexico may be more violet and purple.

Each year, females dip their tails into soft soil and lay up to 100 eggs. As with all grasshopper species, these eggs hatch into tiny versions of the adults. Because these miniature offspring cannot fly, many people call their young "hoppers."

LENGTH: .8–1.4 in.

FOUND IN: Throughout the southern US and into Mexico

DIET: Grasses, shrubs, and trees

HORSEHEAD GRASSHOPPER
(Pseudoproscopia scabra)

With its long sticklike head and barklike camouflage, the horsehead grasshopper is the stick insect of the grasshopper world. It moves among the twigs and branches feeding upon leaves, scanning the treetops for approaching predators using wraparound eyes that allow it to see in all directions at once.

As with other grasshoppers, the horsehead grasshopper senses its surroundings using a pair of special antennae used to touch and smell potential food. Its face is also covered with tiny hairs, which help it detect small changes in its environment.

LENGTH: 5.9–7.9 in.

FOUND IN: Throughout Brazil, French Guiana, Venezuela, and Peru

DIET: Leaves and grasses

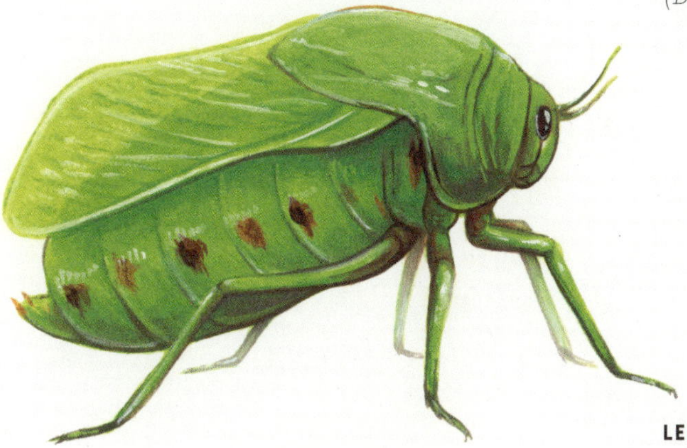

GREEN BLADDER GRASSHOPPER
(Bullacris intermedia)

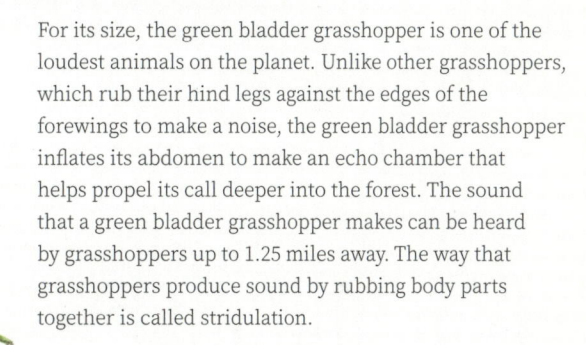

For its size, the green bladder grasshopper is one of the loudest animals on the planet. Unlike other grasshoppers, which rub their hind legs against the edges of the forewings to make a noise, the green bladder grasshopper inflates its abdomen to make an echo chamber that helps propel its call deeper into the forest. The sound that a green bladder grasshopper makes can be heard by grasshoppers up to 1.25 miles away. The way that grasshoppers produce sound by rubbing body parts together is called stridulation.

LENGTH: 1.65–1.9 in.

DIET: Leaves and grasses

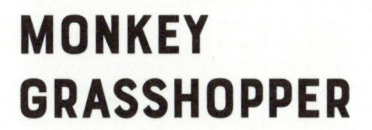

FOUND IN: Savanna and shrublands of southern Africa

MONKEY GRASSHOPPER
(Eumastax vittata)

The monkey grasshopper gets its name from the way it holds its legs outward when resting. Stretched out like this, its legs look a little like those of a monkey.

The monkey grasshopper and its close relatives resemble some of the early grasshoppers that lived in the age of dinosaurs. In the modern day, these grasshoppers still feed on the same plants that existed back then, such as conifers and ferns.

Unlike other grasshoppers, the monkey grasshopper does not possess an eardrum (called a tympanum) with which to hear forest sounds.

LENGTH: .6–.8 in.

DIET: Primitive plants

FOUND IN: Throughout tropical regions of South America

LOCUSTS (ORTHOPTERA)

Locusts are a part of the grasshopper group known for their habit of swarming together in the millions after periods of heavy rain. During these periods, adults and the wingless juveniles (called hoppers) go on the rampage, often damaging human crops in the process.

MIGRATORY LOCUST
(Locusta migratoria)

Like other locusts, the migratory locust doesn't always form vast swarms. Often, the migratory locust prefers to keep away from others of its kind. It is only when food sources become hard to find, causing locusts to compete for food, that individuals change their behavior and their notorious traveling swarms begin to form.

Swarms of migratory locusts move with impressive speed, sometimes traveling more than 80 miles in a single day. During this time, an adult locust will eat more than its own body weight in crops.

LENGTH: 1.6–2.4 in.

DIET: Leaves, flowers, fruits, seeds, plant stems, and bark

FOUND IN: Asia, Africa, Australia, and New Zealand

AUSTRALIAN PLAGUE LOCUST
(Chortoicetes terminifera)

The Australian plague locust is one of many insects that can be eaten by humans once it has been prepared and cooked properly. Some scientists think that the practice of eating insects may become more and more common because locusts cost very little to produce compared to farm animals and their meat is very nutritious. They are said to taste crispy and crunchy.

In some years, the Australian plague locust can cause millions of dollars' worth of damage to farmers' crops and pastures as it moves through their fields feeding in massive swarms.

LENGTH: .8–1.8 in.

DIET: Leaves, flowers, fruits, seeds, plant stems, and bark

FOUND IN: Throughout Australia

DESERT LOCUST

(Schistocerca gregaria)

Few insects affect the lives of human beings quite like the desert locust. In the years in which giant swarms form, 750 million people around the world go without food because of the relentless impact they can have upon our crops.

The secret behind the success of the desert locust is that this species breeds incredibly quickly. Where other insects might go through one generation each year, the desert locust can breed every two months or more, producing hundreds of eggs at a time. This means that, if conditions allow, populations of locusts can skyrocket.

In some years, swarms of desert locusts can form that contain 200 million locusts per sq mile in a cloud of activity almost 750 miles wide, containing billions of locusts in total.

Scientists and farmers have tried many different ways to limit the spread of the desert locust, including digging ditches, spraying the air with chemicals, and even employing the help of special wasps that hunt and kill them. The fight, however, continues.

LENGTH: 1.6–2.4 in.

DIET: Leaves, flowers, fruits, seeds, plant stems, and bark

FOUND IN: Throughout Africa, the Middle East, and Asia

CRICKETS (ORTHOPTERA)

Crickets have cylinder-shaped bodies, round heads, and long antennae. Of 300 species worldwide, many are nocturnal. Crickets have a pair of hard wing-cases, which can be used to make a chirping sound. Long back legs mean that most crickets are very good at jumping.

AUSTRALIAN MOLE CRICKET
(Gryllotalpa brachyptera)

With forelegs like shovels, the Australian mole cricket digs through soil. Its velvetlike hair provides extra protection while it tunnels.

Each year, the male Australian mole cricket constructs a special pit in the ground, which widens at the opening like the mouth of a trumpet. From this pit, he makes his "churring" calls (a whirling or trilling sound)—a noise so loud that it makes the nearby soil shake. This feat makes the Australian mole cricket one of the world's most industrious insects.

LENGTH: Approximately 1.57 in.

DIET: Plant roots and insect larvae

FOUND IN: Damp soils in farmland, parks and bushlands of southeastern Australia

WĒTĀPUNGA
(Deinacrida heteracantha)

The wētāpunga is a very secretive giant cricket that looks for the juiciest leaves in the dead of night. Unlike many crickets, it is totally flightless, though its hindmost legs can provide a springing leap if needed.

Almost the entire world population of wētāpunga lives on a single island near New Zealand where they were once common. Sadly, the introduction of predatory rats has caused this species to disappear. The wētāpunga is now threatened with extinction.

LENGTH: Approximately 2.95 in.

DIET: Leaves

FOUND IN: Forests of Little Barrier Island, off New Zealand

OAK BUSH CRICKET
(Meconema thalassinum)

The oak bush cricket cannot sing like other crickets and so it drums. Males find a suitable leaf or branch and then tap their hind feet to create a low humming noise that travels through the forest. Female oak bush crickets are attracted to these unusual calls.

Like many crickets, the female has a long bladelike bottom called an ovipositor. She uses her ovipositor to glue her eggs to the undersides of leaves. The male (pictured) has a pair of antennae-like feelers called cerci.

LENGTH: .79 in., not including the long antennae

FOUND IN: Woodlands, parklands, and gardens throughout Europe

DIET: Small invertebrates

SPIKED MAGICIAN
(Saga pedo)

The spiked magician gets its name from the strange dance it performs. As it gets closer and closer to its prey, it waves it forelegs rhythmically in the air and attempts to enchant and hypnotize its potential meal. Once it is within range, the spiked magician strikes out with spiny legs like those of a mantis.

The spiked magician is so predatory that it is even known to kill others of its own kind. This may be one of the only crickets known to display cannibalistic behaviors.

LENGTH: Up to 4.72 in.

DIET: Insects

FOUND IN: Meadows and pastures throughout southern Europe and Asia

STICK INSECTS (PHASMATODEA)

Stick insects are hard to study because of their cryptic camouflage, which is unrivaled among insects that live in the forest canopy. Scientists have so far described almost 3,000 different species, though there are likely to be many more undiscovered species out there.

PHRYGANISTRIA CHINENSIS ZHAO

With a body longer than an adult human's arm, *Phryganistria chinensis Zhao* is the world's longest insect. Even its babies are long, measuring .79 in. or more, according to the Chinese scientist who first discovered and named this secretive species in 2016.

Because insects do not have lungs like bony animals, they are limited in their size by how much oxygen they can get into their bodies. For this reason, *Phryganistria chinensis Zhao* may be as big as an insect on planet Earth could ever manage to be.

LENGTH: 24.6 in.

DIET: Leaves

FOUND IN: Mountainous forests of China's Guangxi Zhuang region

DEVIL RIDER
(Anisomorpha buprestoides)

These stick insects are known as "devils" because, when threatened by predators, they can squirt a stinky poison from the underside of their body. This chemical spray is very similar to catnip and may cause some mammals to run away scared.

As with all stick insects, the devil rider often rocks slowly back and forth as it lurks on branches. As well as making the devil rider look like a stick blowing in the wind, this behavior also helps its eyes gather a three-dimensional view of its surroundings.

LENGTH: 1.6–2.6 in.

DIET: Leaves

FOUND IN: Throughout the southeastern US

GOLIATH STICK INSECT
(Eurycnema goliath)

When cornered by a predator, the goliath stick insect gives off a dramatic warning. It opens up its wings and shows off bright bands of color to make itself look big and scary. It can also make a loud and intimidating hiss like a snake. For this reason, many predators think twice before attacking the goliath stick insect.

Like many stick insects, the female goliath stick insect can produce babies without the need for a male—this is called parthenogenesis. When produced like this, the goliath stick insect's hatchlings grow to become identical copies (or clones) of their mother.

Goliath stick insect eggs are often flicked onto the ground. There, the eggs are picked up by hungry ants who mistake them for seeds and take them back to their nest. In the nest, the baby stick insect hatches in safety before climbing up the nearest tree to start a new life in the forest canopy.

LENGTH: Up to 9.8 in.

DIET: Eucalyptus trees and acacias

FOUND IN: Across many parts of the eastern coast of Australia

STONEFLIES (PLECOPTERA)

The scientific name for stoneflies (Plecoptera) means "braided-wing." This is because nearly all of the world's 3,500 stonefly species have very striking patterns of veins on their wings. Stoneflies are an incredibly ancient part of the insect group. Their ancestors thrived more than 100 million years before dinosaurs.

OTWAY STONEFLY
(Eusthenia nothofagi)

The mysterious otway stonefly was thought to have faced extinction until, in 1991, scientists rediscovered it living in the forest streams of eastern Australia. Today, sightings of this stonefly are incredibly rare, making this one of the hardest-to-find insects in the world.

The otway stonefly came close to extinction because its forest habitats were being cleared at a faster and faster rate. It was also affected by unpredictable weather caused by climate change. These weather events can damage its remote habitat more quickly than the species can adapt.

LENGTH: Approximately 1.57 in.

FOUND IN: Forest streams of Victoria, Australia

DIET: Aquatic nymphs are predators of tiny invertebrates

COMMON YELLOW SALLY
(Isoperla grammatica)

Like nearly all stoneflies, the baby life stage (nymph) of the common yellow sally lives in fast-flowing streams where it hides under rocks and pebbles. Its nymphs do not have well-developed gills and therefore they have to absorb oxygen directly into their bodies through tiny holes.

When the nymphs of the common yellow sally reach the later stages of their development, they creep to the edge of the stream and climb up nearby plants. They then shed their skin and fly away in their adult form.

LENGTH: Approximately .39 in.

FOUND IN: Common near fast-flowing streams of Europe and North America

DIET: Omnivorous—plankton, algae, and other microorganisms

KNOBBED SALMONFLY
(Pteronarcys biloba)

The nymphs of the knobbed salmonfly are an important source of food for salmon, hence their name. In the millions, the nymphs chew through leaf litter on the bottom of fast-flowing streams. When salmon approach, the nymphs immediately freeze and hope they can avoid being spotted.

Knobbed salmonfly emerge as adults in late May and June. Like all stoneflies, adult knobbed salmonfly have very simple mouthparts that can be used to nibble plants to top up their energy reserves while finding a mate and laying their eggs.

LENGTH: 1.6–2 in.

DIET: Leaves and decaying leaf matter

FOUND IN: Fast-moving streams throughout North America

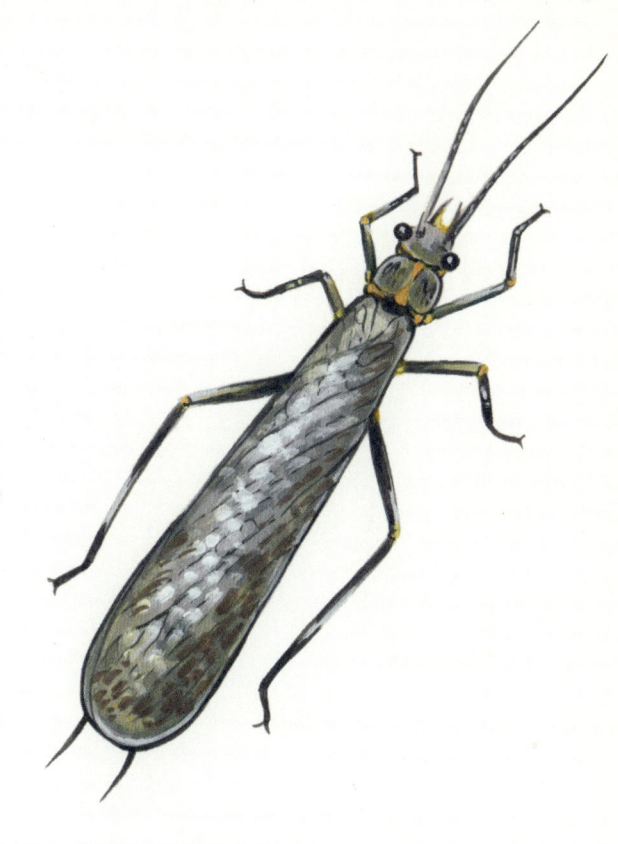

ALASKAN STONEFLY
(Nemoura arctica)

The Alaskan stonefly is one of the only insects that can stand being frozen solid. When frozen, its cells don't freeze and shatter like the cells of other insects because it fills them with a sugary antifreeze liquid as the water around it cools. Laboratory studies suggest that the Alaskan stonefly can survive for weeks on end trapped in icy waters below 14 °F. This adaptation helps the Alaskan stonefly survive the winter months in the Alaskan streams in which it lives.

LENGTH: .3–.4 in.

DIET: Leaf material

FOUND IN: Fast-flowing streams of Alaska

EARWIGS (DERMAPTERA)

Earwigs are known for the pincers on the tip of their abdomen and their tough armored forewings. Approximately 2,000 species are known from every continent on Earth except Antarctica. Most earwigs are active only at night, when they move out from moist crevices and caves to search for food.

LINED EARWIG
(Doru taeniatum)

Like many earwigs, the lined earwig can raise its forked pincerlike tail to defend itself from attack. But the lined earwig has another defensive trick up its sleeve. When threatened, it shoots out jets of foul-smelling yellow goo from its body. Many predators find the smell and taste of this fluid disgusting and leave the lined earwig alone.

Males and females can be told apart from each other by the shape of their tails. Males have curved pincers and females have straight ones.

LENGTH: .55–.7 in.

DIET: Omnivorous

FOUND IN: Grasslands and forests throughout Central America, North America, and South America

COMMON EARWIG
(Forficula auricularia)

The common earwig is a very good mother to her babies. She tends to her eggs throughout the winter months, keeping them spotlessly clean. When her babies hatch, she will look after them for weeks on end, protecting them from predators in her underground burrow.

Although the common earwig has wings, it rarely uses them and they are very hard to see. When unfolded, the wings look a little bit like a pair of human ears—this is where earwigs get their name.

LENGTH: .47–.59 in.

DIET: Omnivorous

FOUND IN: Across Asia, Europe and North Africa; introduced to North America

GIANT MURID RAT EARWIG

(Hemimerus hanseni)

Hemimerus hanseni and other species of giant murid rat earwig spend their whole lives clinging onto the fur of giant African rats. To hold on tight, its legs are covered with tiny grooves. For many years, scientists were unsure whether this earwig feasted upon the rats' skin or the rats' blood. By closely inspecting its mouthparts, scientists think it probably eats dead skin and fungus.

Unlike other earwigs, the giant murid earwig gives birth to tiny babies that hatch from eggs within its body.

LENGTH: .2–.59 in.

DIET: Dead skin and fungus

FOUND IN: Upon giant pouched rats of sub-Saharan Africa

ST HELENA GIANT EARWIG

(Labidura herculeana)

Almost as big as a medium-sized scorpion, the St Helena giant earwig is recognized as one of the world's largest earwigs. After rain, it is said to emerge from its deep burrow to search for food scraps among the seabird colonies of its remote island home.

Once common on the island of St Helena in the south Atlantic Ocean, the giant earwig appears to have disappeared in recent centuries. A living specimen has not been seen for more than 50 years, leading scientists to suspect that it is now extinct. The hunt, however, continues.

LENGTH: Up to 3.3 in.

DIET: Omnivorous

FOUND IN: Plains, gumwood forests, and seabird colonies across the oceanic island of St Helena

MANTISES (MANTODEA)

With impressive jaws, superb vision, and raptorlike claws, mantises are supreme hunters. Nearly all species are ambush predators, striking at small animals that fail to spot them and stray too close. Around 2,400 species live in habitats around the world.

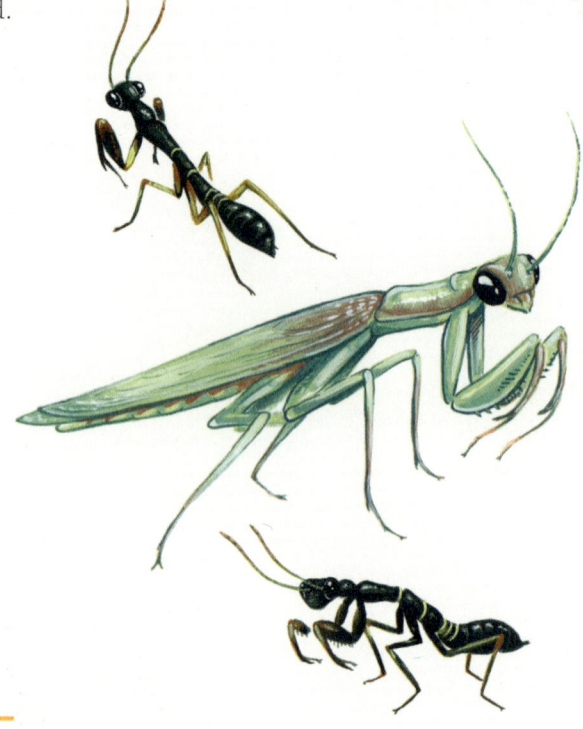

WALKING FLOWER MANTIS
(Hymenopus coronatus)

The walking flower mantis has broad legs that look like orchid petals and its color matches almost perfectly the flowers to which it has adapted. For most insects, camouflage like this helps keeps an individual safe from predators, but the walking flower mantis is hiding from something else—its prey.

Perfectly camouflaged, the walking flower mantis sits at the edge of a flower. When a nectar-thirsty bee or fly visits, assuming it to be a flower, the mantis flicks out its spiky legs to impale its prey.

LENGTH: Females up to 2.36 in.; males up to 1.57 in.

FOUND IN: Throughout the rainforests of Indonesia

DIET: Insects including crickets, flies, beetles, wasps, and bees

ASIAN ANT MANTIS
(Odontomantis planiceps)

The Asian ant mantis gets its name from its young nymphs, which look exactly like ants. This mimicry is so good that many predators leave these baby mantises alone, assuming them to be poisonous or capable of biting.

As they grow, mantis nymphs need to shed their skins. A mantis may need to shed its skin eight times or more to reach its adult size, at which point it may lay hundreds of eggs, which it glues to the underside of leaves in a little capsule.

LENGTH: .98 in.

FOUND IN: Rainforests of Southeast Asia

DIET: Small invertebrates

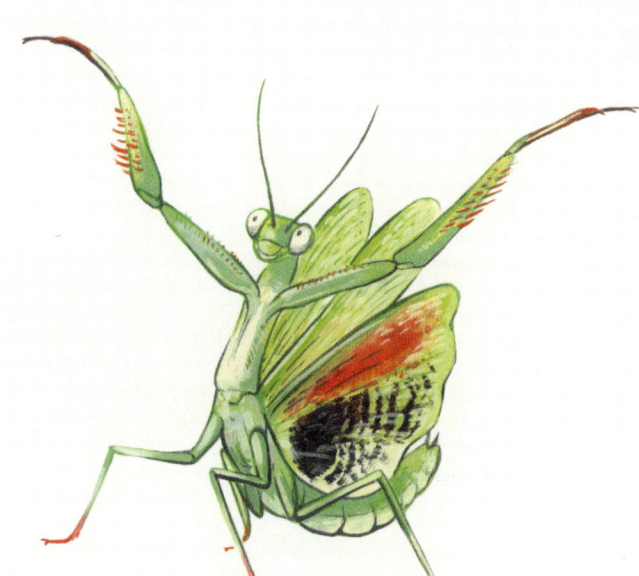

MEDITERRANEAN MANTIS
(Iris oratoria)

Most predators know not to attack the Mediterranean mantis. When it feels threatened, this mantis goes face-to-face with its attacker, arches its back like a scorpion and waves its knifelike forelegs aggressively. This species can also raise its wings like a cape upon which bright eyespots are painted—these eyespots trick some predators into thinking a bigger predator has suddenly appeared.

Like a grasshopper, the Mediterranean mantis is also capable of making noise. It scrapes its wings together to make a scratching sound.

LENGTH: 2.56 in.

DIET: Insects, including bees and grasshoppers

FOUND IN: Throughout Europe; introduced to the Middle East, Asia, and the US

CHINESE MANTIS
(Tenodera sinensis)

The Chinese mantis is capable of killing and eating species much larger and heavier than itself, including hummingbirds and dragonflies. To catch fast-moving prey like this, the Chinese mantis depends on huge eyes that are widely spaced apart. This gives them excellent binocular vision, helping them make their kill first time.

Like many mantises, the Chinese mantis regularly eats others of its own species. Females are well-known for eating males after mating has occurred.

LENGTH: Up to 4.33 in.

DIET: Mostly spiders, grasshoppers and flying insects; occasionally larger prey such as hummingbirds

FOUND IN: China, Japan, the Korean Peninsula and Thailand; accidentally released into parts of the US where it now thrives

COCKROACHES AND TERMITES (BLATTODEA)

Termites and cockroaches are closely related to each other in a group called the Blattodea. They are very social and communicate with each other through smell, touch, and taste. In the case of termites, vast colonies are built where a single egg-laying queen is responsible for creating an army of workers.

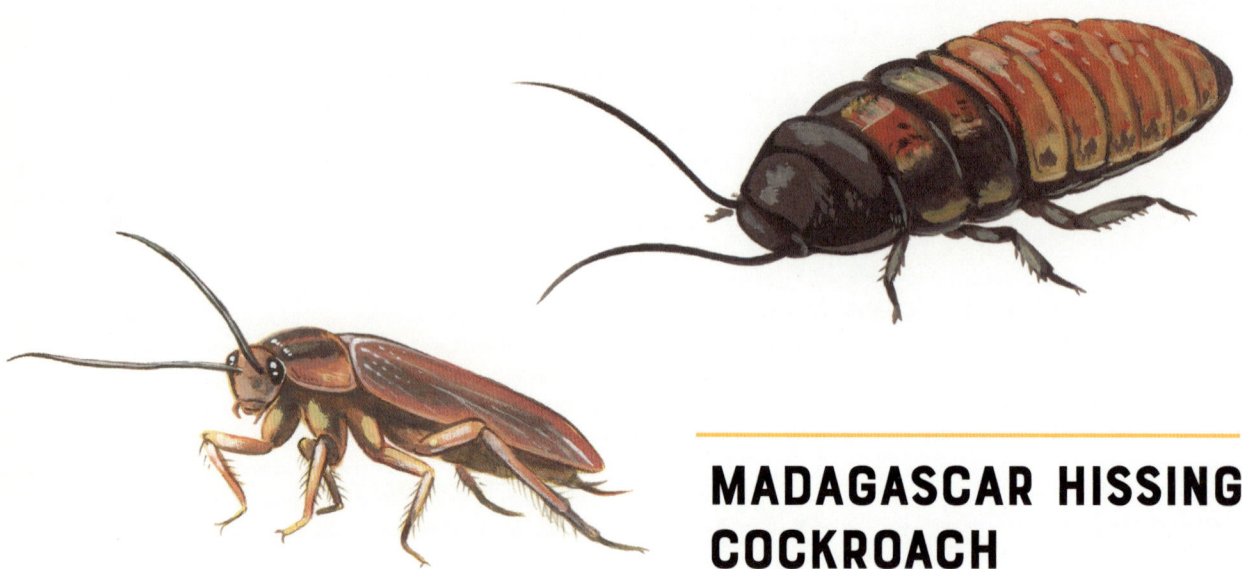

GERMAN COCKROACH
(Blattella germanica)

The German cockroach is one of the world's most troublesome cockroaches. Though it usually likes scraps of meat and sweet foods, it is capable of eating many household items, including glue, soap, and toothpaste. This means it can thrive in towns and cities.

One of the main reasons for the success of cockroaches is the speed they can grow. Just 60 days after hatching from its egg, the German cockroach begins producing its own babies. This means its numbers can swell very quickly.

LENGTH: .4–.6 in.

DIET: Omnivorous—able to eat most foods

FOUND IN: Once a European and Asian species, the German cockroach has now spread to all continents except Antarctica

MADAGASCAR HISSING COCKROACH
(Gromphadorhina portentosa)

By forcing air out of small holes on its abdomen, this large cockroach can hiss loudly to scare away predators. Males also use their hissing to attract the attention of nearby females, like a bird singing.

As with many cockroaches, the female Madagascar hissing cockroach keeps her developing eggs in an egg-packet (called an ootheca) within her body. Her babies hatch within the ootheca and then climb out of her body to begin their life in the busy Madagascan rainforest.

LENGTH: 2–3 in.

DIET: Omnivorous

FOUND IN: Often found hiding in dead logs within Madagascan rainforests

MACROTERMES GILVUS

Termite societies are ruled by a king and a queen, who are responsible for the colony growing in numbers. Their babies hatch into workers, which find food for the colony, or soldiers, which are responsible for the nest's protection.

Queens lay many, many eggs in their lifetime, and *Macrotermes gilvus* is among the most prolific. Her body swells to such a size that she cannot move and so her workers help her birth her eggs. In a single day, she can lay thousands of eggs.

LENGTH: Workers .47–.6 in.; queens approximately 2.4 in.

FOUND IN: Throughout Southeast Asia

DIET: Omnivorous

SYNTERMES DIRUS

Syntermes dirus is the most industrious engineer on the planet. In the last few thousand years, this single species has built more than 200 million termite nests (called mounds) across Brazil, spanning an area the size of Great Britain.

In total, the amount of soil moved by these impressive termites to build their nests is equivalent to the amount that would be needed to create 4,000 Great Pyramids of Giza. Not bad for an insect no bigger than a child's thumbnail.

LENGTH: .4–.6 in.

FOUND IN: Rainforest and grassland across northeastern Brazil

DIET: Omnivorous

BOOKLICE (PSOCOPTERA)

Booklice were first known for their habit of eating the glue used to bind old books, hence the name. However, scientists have since discovered that there are thousands of species, many more than once imagined. In all, 4,500 species are currently known, only a handful of which have a common name.

WEB-SPINNING BARKLOUSE
(Archipsocus nomas)

The web-spinning barklouse fires silk from out of its mouth, rather than the tip of its abdomen like a spider. By moving its head back and forth while spraying, it makes a silken blanket that protects its developing eggs from predators. When lots of web-spinning barklice share a tree together, their combined silk-spinning can cover the tree in silvery webbing.

Like a spider, this species can respond to the vibrations of larger predators walking upon the surface of its silk cave. When it feels movement above, it quickly hides.

LENGTH: .12 in.   **FOUND IN:** Southeastern US

DIET: Algae and lichens

LIPOSCELIS BOSTRYCHOPHILA

This tiny booklouse has hitchhiked its way across all parts of the world by stowing away in shipments of cereals, its favorite food. The secret to its success is that females can produce eggs without the need for males—a common trick used by many insects and some other animals.

Like many booklice, *Liposcelis bostrychophila* is wingless. It makes up for this by having long and slender legs, which allow it to climb around on its food. Sturdy mouthparts break up food items before swallowing.

LENGTH: .04 in.   **FOUND IN:** Cereal stores throughout the world

DIET: Cereals

MESOPSOCUS UNIPUNCTATUS

To find this secretive booklouse, scientists put a large white sheet under a tree and then shake the branches to investigate what falls out. It is believed to feed on lichens, which it finds in the cracks among the bark of various tree species.

Mesopsocus unipunctatus is one of a handful of insects known to have changed the colors of its camouflage during the Industrial Revolution, when air pollution killed lichens on trees and made tree trunks less green. During this time, their camouflage went from green to brown.

LENGTH: 1–1.5 in.

DIET: Lichens

FOUND IN: Forests and woodlands across Europe and parts of North America

LIPOSCELIS DIVINATORIUS

In the depths of night, *Liposcelis divinatorius* makes its journey through collections of dusty old books. With its keen senses, it searches out the books held together with delicious glue. Unlike many booklice, the eyes of *Liposcelis divinatorius* are small and simple. It has little need for them—the inside of a closed book is very dark.

To communicate with one another *Liposcelis divinatorius* is able to create sounds by tapping the tip of its abdomen against the floor. For this reason, though they are insects, some people call them "ticking spiders."

LENGTH: .04 in.

DIET: Various human food sources, including grain stores

FOUND IN: In or near human habitations across the world

LICE (PHTHIRAPTERA)

Organisms that steal a living from other organisms are called parasites. Lice are one of the world's most successful parasites. Of nearly 5,000 known species, nearly all of them live on birds and mammals. Lice can be split into two groups: those that eat flakes of skin (the chewing lice) and those that drink blood (the sucking lice).

HEAD LOUSE
(Pediculus humanus capitis)

To hold on to human hair, the head louse has legs that are equipped with little claws that provide a handy grip. These claws make walking along hard surfaces very difficult and so most head lice will travel between humans only when their heads connect with one another and their hairs become briefly entwined.

Head louse eggs are called nits. A female may lay five or six eggs each day. Each of these eggs is laid separately and glued to a single thread of hair to keep it safe.

LENGTH: .1–.12 in.

FOUND IN: Upon humans throughout the world

DIET: Human blood

GOPHER CHEWING LOUSE
(Geomydoecus coronadoi)

Gophers are rodents that live in busy networks of tunnels underground. Many gophers have an unfortunate houseguest—the gopher chewing louse. These parasites make a living by chewing off flakes of the gopher's skin. To do this, the gopher chewing lice have wide heads complete with powerful munching jaws.

Geomydoecus coronadoi is especially common upon Merriam's pocket gopher, a Mexican rodent. Its brown color helps it to hide within the gopher's fur, making it harder for the gopher to spot while it cleans itself.

LENGTH: .04 in.

FOUND IN: Upon the pouched gophers of North and Central America

DIET: Flakes of skin

BROWN BEAR LOUSE
(Trichodectes pinguis)

When a mother bear cuddles up with her newly born cubs, the brown bear louse sees its opportunity to find a new host. It climbs from the mother bear onto a cub, where it will spend its whole life feeding upon the cub's dead skin.

In some cases, the brown bear louse can breed in such numbers that bears can become bald from scratching too much. Without their warm blanket of fur, scientists worry that lice-ridden bears may die in cold weather.

LENGTH: .08 in.

DIET: Flakes of skin

FOUND IN: Upon brown bears across North America and parts of Europe

GOOSE BODY LOUSE
(Trinoton anserinum)

The goose body louse is so fast that some scientists call it a running louse. It runs across the body of swans or geese, weaving in between the feathers looking for patches of rosy skin to feed on.

To penetrate the bird's layer of skin, the goose body louse has jaws that have interlocking serrations that fit together a bit like the teeth of a crocodile. These help it to nibble through the skin to get to the nutritious blood below.

LENGTH: .2–.24 in.

DIET: Blood and skin flakes

FOUND IN: Upon swans and geese across the world

THRIPS (THYSANOPTERA)

Being around a millimeter or less in length, most thrips are very easy to miss. These cylinder-shaped insects feed using a lopsided pair of jaws that can be used to slice into plants and, sometimes, other animals. Worldwide, more than 6,000 species are known.

MELON THRIPS
(Thrips palmi)

Farmers around the world live in fear of the melon thrips. As it feeds, it leaves little scars on the fruit, meaning the fruit cannot then be sold. In heavy infestations, whole fields of crops can be ruined.

Like other species, the melon thrips is capable of flight. Thrips launch into the air by flapping their wings in a manner that is unique to insects. Each waft of their wings creates tiny vortices of air that pull them upward and forward—this is known as "clap and fling" flight.

LENGTH: .03–.04 in.

DIET: Stems, leaves, and fruit

FOUND IN: Originally Southeast Asia; now worldwide

MIROTHRIPS ARBITER

Many thrips are parasites of other species, but few take a risk quite like the *Mirothrips arbiter*. This tiny thrips species spends its whole life entrenched within the bustling nests of busy wasps, often alongside thousands of other thrips. Together, these thrips ransack the eggs of these wasps, sometimes killing the entire nest of wasps in the process.

So far, this tiny thrips has been found in the nests of three different wasp species, but scientists suspect they are likely to find many more as they continue their search.

LENGTH: .04–.08 in.

DIET: Wasp eggs

FOUND IN: Paper wasp nests in Brazil

KLADOTHRIPS INTERMEDIUS

Like ants, wasps, bees, and termites, the *Kladothrips intermedius* lives in a nest ruled by a queen who is in charge of producing eggs. From these eggs, different types (or castes) of babies emerge—some will become workers that help tend to the eggs and find food, while others (the soldiers) keep the nest safe from attack.

Females of this species create nests by biting into branches of umbrella bush and squirting in a special chemical that causes the tree to create a protective growth (called a gall) in which she can live in safety.

LENGTH: .04 in.

DIET: Acacia leaves

FOUND IN: Arid and semiarid regions of Australia

THRIPS SETIPENNIS

Though it has never been given a common name, *Thrips setipennis* has a lot of responsibility. This species is the only insect able to pollinate a species of tree called brush muttonwood that grows in eastern Australia. Without the thrips, this tree would eventually die out.

Many thrips move pollen around in this way and form a lifelong relationship with specific plant species. In fact, some scientists think that thrips may have pollinated flowers long before bees were around, millions of years ago.

LENGTH: Approximately .04 in.

DIET: Nectar from flowers

FOUND IN: Eastern parts of Australia

WATER BUGS (HEMIPTERA)

Water bugs belong to a group called the hemipterans (also known as "true bugs") which have beetle-like bodies and pointed mouthparts that can be stabbed into plants or animals in order to suck up nutritious juices. Most water bugs are predatory.

WATER STICK INSECT
(Ranatra linearis)

Like an underwater mantis, the water stick insect (which is actually a bug) hides itself among underwater weeds and grasses and waits for prey such as tadpoles and tiny fish to stray too close. Once prey has been seized, its pointed mouthparts inject chemicals into its meal, which turn the prey's cells into a digestible soup. After waiting a few moments, the water stick insect then begins to suck up its nutritious catch.

LENGTH: Up to 2 in.

DIET: Tadpoles, small fish, water fleas and insect larvae

FOUND IN: Ponds and lakes throughout Europe, Asia and North Africa

COMMON BACKSWIMMER
(Notonecta glauca)

The common backswimmer cruises the open waters of ponds and lakes like a shark. Unusually for water bugs, it swims completely upside down with only its abdomen poking out of the water. This means it can pull oxygen into its bottom while at the same time scanning the waters below for potential prey.

The common backswimmer propels itself forward using two elongated legs that look a little like oars on a boat—for this reason, some people call this species the "greater water boatman."

LENGTH: .5–.63 in.

DIET: Freshwater invertebrates, as well as tadpoles and small fish

FOUND IN: Common to ponds and lakes across Europe, North Africa and Asia

TOE BITER
(Lethocerus americanus)

This enormous water bug gets it name from its habit of biting humans if stepped on or handled roughly. Its bite comes from pointed mouthparts normally used like a drinking straw to suck out juices from prey, which it holds in place using impressively muscled forelegs.

Like all water bugs, the toe biter has wings and is capable of flying. At night, it is often drawn to electric lights such as streetlamps, which it mistakes for a full moon. Scientists are concerned that this drains its energy reserves and leads to it becoming lost.

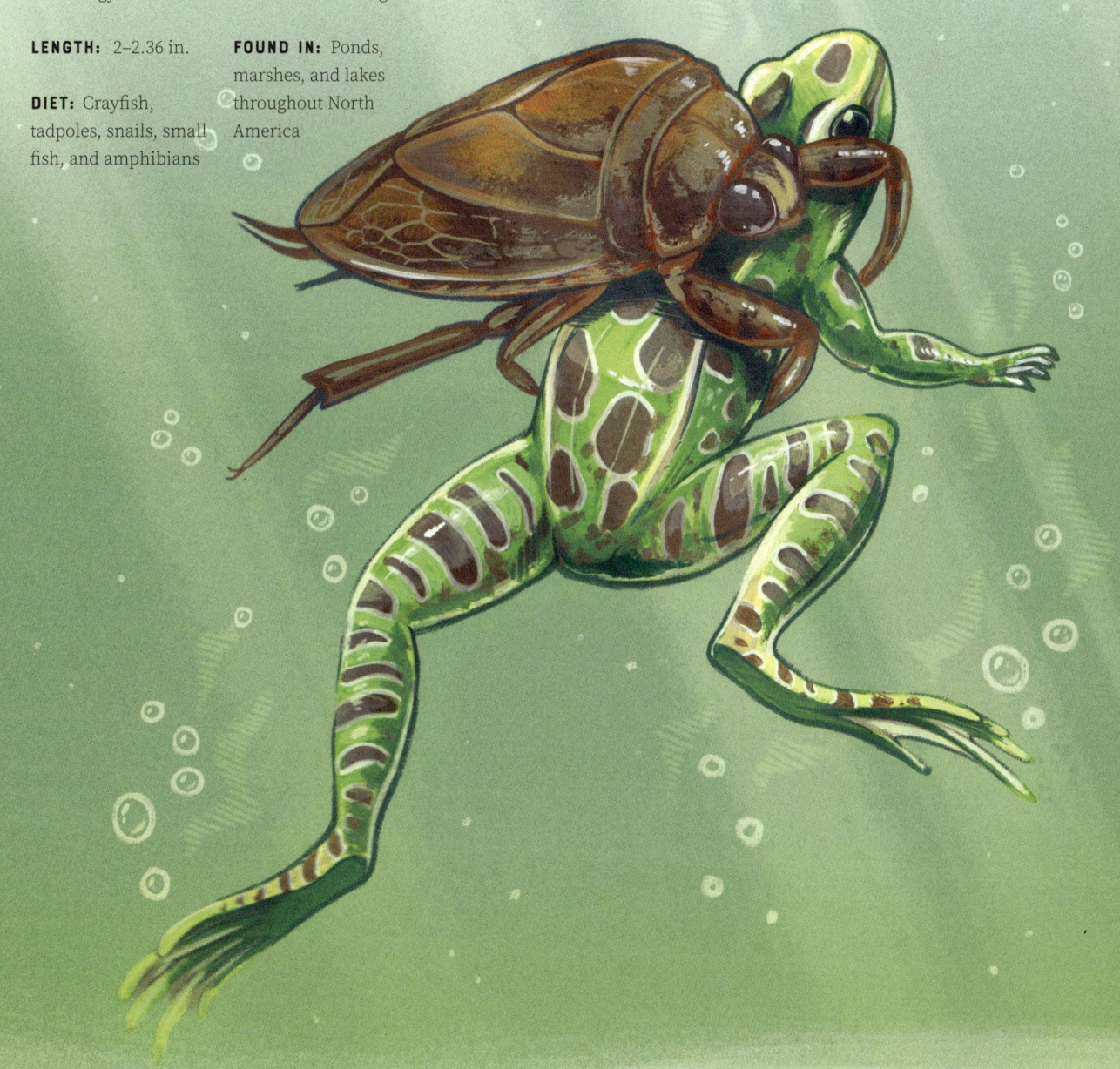

LENGTH: 2–2.36 in.

DIET: Crayfish, tadpoles, snails, small fish, and amphibians

FOUND IN: Ponds, marshes, and lakes throughout North America

CICADAS (HEMIPTERA)

More than 3,000 of these sap-drinking bugs are known from forests and grasslands. The largest members of this group include the cicadas, which are famous for their loud churring songs. Smaller members include the insects known as froghoppers and treehoppers.

PHARAOH CICADA
(Magicicada septendecim)

No one is quite sure how, but the pharaoh nymph is able to count. It spends years of its life as an underground nymph, counting the years that go by before, in its 17th year, emerging as an adult along with thousands of others. So many adult cicadas emerge at once, that predators such as birds and mammals are unable to eat them all. This clever tactic means that some pharaoh cicadas survive and the 17-year cycle can continue.

LENGTH: 1.57 in.

FOUND IN: Canada and the US

DIET: Sap from trees

AUSTRALIAN GREENGROCER
(Cyclochila australasiae)

The Australian greengrocer is one of the world's loudest insects. Occasionally its calls reach 150 decibels, approaching the noise levels of a blue whale. To make these calls, male greengrocers flex riblike structures on their body. A special resonating chamber makes the call travel extra far.

As with other cicadas, the colors of the Australian greengrocer can vary. Some forms are turquoise (called "blue moons" by local people) and some are yellow (called "yellow Mondays"). Many insects have different local forms like this. These forms are called "morphs."

LENGTH: 1.57 in.

FOUND IN: Coastal parts of southeastern Australia

DIET: Sap from trees

MEADOW FROGHOPPER
(Philaenus spumarius)

The scientific name for this species of bug translates to "foam-lover" because of the strange behavior of the nymphs, which excrete bubbly liquid from their bottoms as they feed on plant sap. This foam stops the nymph from drying up as it grows, as well as protecting it from passing predators.

The adult meadow froghopper is capable of spectacular jumps for its size. In the blink of an eye, it can leap 2 feet or more. Though this compares with the jumping ability of fleas, the meadow froghopper manages this incredible leap with a body 60 times heavier.

LENGTH: .2–.28 in.

DIET: Sap from a range of plants

FOUND IN: Throughout Europe, Asia and North Africa

BRAZILIAN TREEHOPPER
(Bocydium globulare)

The Brazilian treehopper is hard to spot. While it feeds on the undersides of leaves, it holds its body still like a statue.

No one is quite sure why this species has a strange ball-covered growth sticking out from its back. Some scientists think that this unusual protrusion may be a decoy, meaning that hungry birds bite this area rather than eat the treehopper's body beneath. Other scientists argue that the fine covering of hairs may be used to sense for nearby predators or make the treehopper harder for predators to swallow.

LENGTH: .2–.3 in.

DIET: Sap from leaves

FOUND IN: Throughout Africa, North and South America, Asia, and Australia

ASSASSIN BUGS (HEMIPTERA)

The assassin bugs are a large family of hemipterans with a taste for other insects. With a sturdy body and strong legs, they overpower their prey before piercing their exoskeleton with a knifelike beak called a rostrum.

AUSTRALIAN COMMON ASSASSIN BUG

(Pristhesancus plagipennis)

This assassin bug is often called the "bee-killer" for its habit of hunting honey bees. First it uses its powerful rostrum to stab its prey, and then it injects chemicals that melt the internal organs. The bee's insides become a digestible soup, which the assassin bug later sucks up.

As with many assassin bugs, the Australian common assassin bug can deliver a painful bite if handled by humans. Some predators, such as geckos, choose to leave them alone.

LENGTH: .9 in.

FOUND IN: Throughout Australia

DIET: Honey bees and other insects

ACANTHASPIS PETAX

This African assassin bug has hit upon a peculiar strategy to scare away predators. After it catches an ant and empties it of its internal fluids, it attaches the dead ant's exoskeleton to its abdomen to create a suit of ghoulish armor. In some cases, up to 20 dead ants may be glued to a single adult assassin bug.

This "suit of ants" may be especially useful for scaring away spiders, which are the main predators of *Acanthaspis petax*. The behavior also offers the bug protection by way of camouflage.

LENGTH: .4 in.

DIET: Ants

FOUND IN: East African countries, including Uganda, Kenya, and Tanzania

THREAD-LEGGED BUG
(Ploiaria domestica)

At first glance, the thread-legged bug looks half spider and half praying mantis. The first pair of legs are equipped with sharp spikes and talons, which it uses to strike at and grapple with prey. Forelegs like this are termed "raptorial." The thread-legged bug walks upon its rear-most two pairs of legs.

This species is closely related to other thread-legged bugs in a family called the Emesinae. Scientists are trying to learn more about the Emesinae, a group that contains roughly 900 species worldwide.

LENGTH: Body length of .4 in.

FOUND IN: Urban and suburban areas across southern Europe to Asia

DIET: Spiders and other insects

KISSING BUG
(Rhodnius prolixus)

The kissing bug is the vampire of the assassin bug group. It climbs aboard birds and mammals and stabs its sharp mouthparts into their skin, swallowing a mouthful of blood which it uses to power its growth. Kissing bugs favor the mouths of their victims, where the blood is often near the surface of the skin. It is from this habit that they get their name.

Of 130 species of kissing bug, *Rhodnius prolixus* is the one most dangerous to humans because, as it moves from host to host, it spreads an illness called Chagas disease.

LENGTH: Up to 1.34 in.

FOUND IN: Throughout South America

DIET: Blood

SHIELD BUGS AND JEWEL BUGS (HEMIPTERA)

GIANT SHIELD BUG

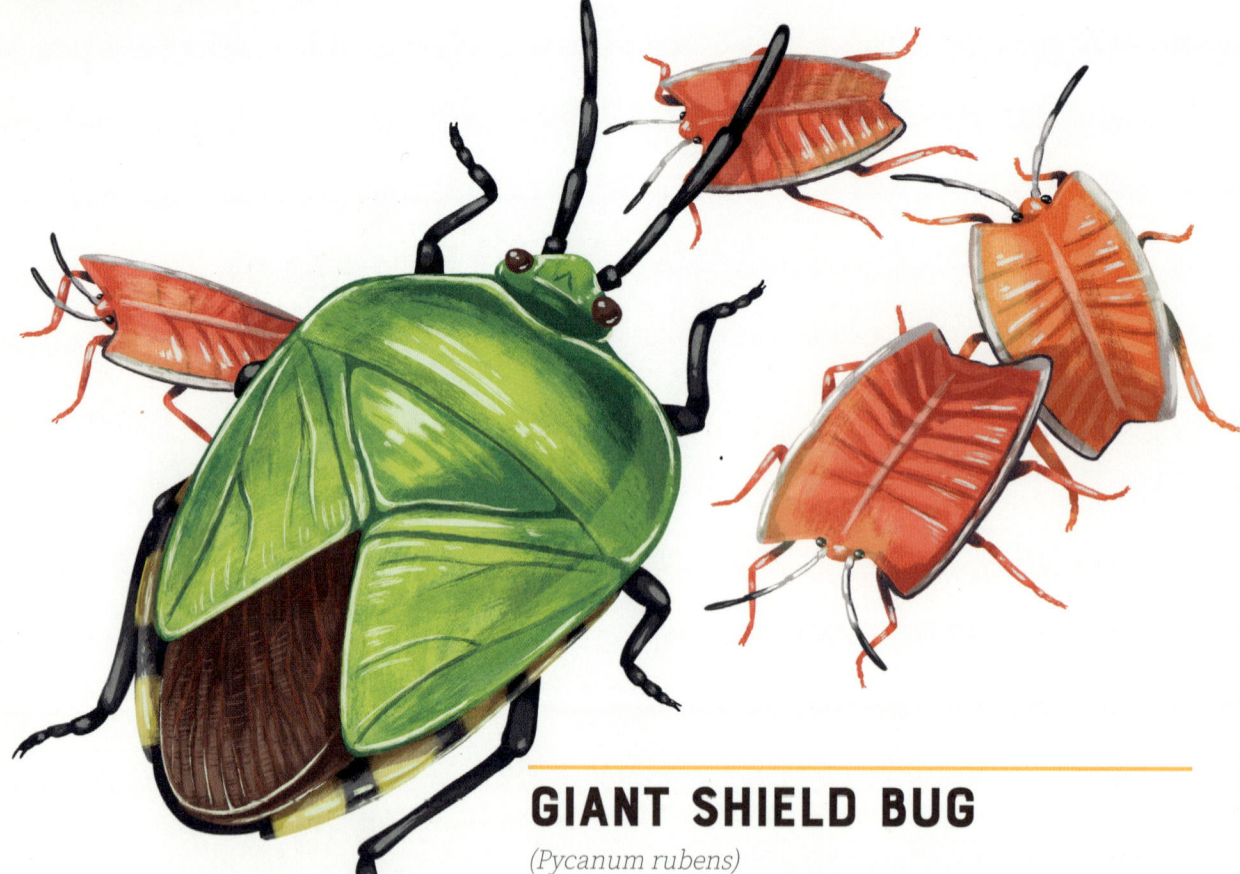

(Pycanum rubens)

Like other shield bugs, the giant shield bug can produce an incredibly overpowering chemical spray if disturbed. This explains the other common name for this insect group—the stink bugs. As well as a bad smell, many species produce chemical compounds that can also temporarily blind mammals or birds when deliberately sprayed into their eyes. Some giant stink bugs can squirt liquid from a distance of almost a foot.

This defensive adaptation scares off most predators, except for their mortal enemy—the parasitic wasp, which searches forests specifically looking for them. These wasps lay their eggs in the body of the giant shield bug and then their grubs eat the bug alive.

Young of the giant shield bug look very different from the adults. To blend into their surroundings, their exoskeleton is covered with markings that mimic the veins on the underside of a leaf. This helps camouflage them until their development into the adult life stage.

LENGTH: Up to 1.2 in.

FOUND IN: Rainforests of Asia

DIET: Sap from tree leaves and stems

METALLIC JEWEL BUG
(Scutiphora pedicellata)

Like others within its family, the male metallic jewel bug uses its shiny colors to show off its health and vigor to females. These beautiful colors are made through thousands of tiny bobbles in the bug's skin, which bend light into a range of shimmering greens and reds.

Occasionally, hundreds of metallic jewel bugs cluster together when threatened by predators. Scientists think that, by teaming up like this, the metallic jewel bug can produce a toxic cloud of gases enough to scare away the threat.

LENGTH: .59 in.

DIET: Plant juices

FOUND IN: Eastern coast of Australia, including Tasmania

PARENT BUG
(Elasmucha grisea)

The parent bug gets its name from its spectacular devotion to childcare. As the eggs hatch, parent bug nymphs eat the eggshells, which the mother has covered in special gut bacteria that the young nymphs require to digest plant juices later in life.

As her young continue to grow, the mother marches them from feeding plant to feeding plant, guiding their movement with her antennae. Only on their third molt will the young juveniles leave her care to begin a life of their own.

LENGTH: Up to .35 in.

DIET: Plant juices from trees including beech, alder, and holly

FOUND IN: Common throughout woodlands in most of Europe

APHIDS (HEMIPTERA)

What the aphids and scale insects lack in size, they make up for in sheer numbers. By cloning themselves and giving birth to identical copies of themselves again and again, whole trees can become full of their offspring. This means that some aphid species can become serious pests of plants.

DARK GREEN NETTLE APHID
(Aphis urticata)

To prosper, dark green nettle aphids need ants to scare away their predators. To befriend them, the dark green nettle aphid produces from its bottom a sticky globule of sweet liquid (called honeydew) that gives a sugary reward to hungry ants. In return for this sugar, the ants protect whole colonies of aphids, guarding them from predators such as ladybugs and their larvae.

Some ant species carefully gather aphid eggs and keep them safe over winter, returning them back to their food plants in the spring months to hatch safely.

LENGTH: Up to .09 in.

DIET: Plant juices from nettles

FOUND IN: Woodlands and grasslands across Europe and Asia

BOOGIE-WOOGIE APHID
(Grylloprociphilus imbricator)

The boogie-woogie aphid gets its name from a defensive behavior unlike any other in the insect world. When threatened, this fluff-covered aphid rears up onto its legs and sways its bottom in the air rhythmically as if in a trance. Thousands of neighboring aphids join this strange performance, creating a blanket of aphids moving in unison together. The movement of thousands and thousands of dancing aphids creates a rippling effect through the branches of the trees that confuses and scares off predators.

LENGTH: .08–.16 in.

FOUND IN: The US

DIET: The sap of American beech trees

WHEAT APHID
(Schizaphis graminum)

Like many aphids, the female wheat aphid is born pregnant with babies that are identical copies (or clones) of herself. Within days of her birth, she begins laying her own tiny nymphs—sometimes at a rate of five a day. This ability to make clones means that aphid populations can skyrocket in only a matter of days, covering leaves and twigs.

Only in autumn do females begin laying a batch of winged aphids that are male. These male aphids fertilize the remaining females, which lay eggs that are glued to trees over winter.

LENGTH: .05–.09 in.

DIET: Sap from a range of grass species

FOUND IN: Throughout temperate parts of the Northern Hemisphere

GIANT WILLOW APHID
(Tuberolachnus salignus)

The giant willow aphid is one of the world's largest and most mysterious aphids. Even though the species is common throughout the Northern Hemisphere, there is much that scientists are still trying to discover.

Firstly, unlike other aphid species, no males have ever been found. Secondly, unlike other aphids, giant willow aphids possess a sharklike dorsal fin with no obvious purpose. Lastly, though they are active in winter and autumn, they seem to completely disappear between March and August. Where they go during this time is unknown.

LENGTH: .2–.24 in.

DIET: Sap of the willow tree

FOUND IN: All continents on Earth, except Australasia and Antarctica

MOSS BUGS AND SCALE INSECTS (HEMIPTERA)

Moss bugs and scale insects are small and easy-to-overlook hemipterans. Most species move very little, staying as still as possible while feeding on plant juices so as not to draw attention to themselves. Scale insects are known for their shell-like coverings, often made of a waxy substance.

JUMPING MOSS BUG
(Hackeriella veitchi)

The spectacular leap of a jumping moss bug rivals that of a flea or a treehopper. By springing off its hind legs, it can lift off at a staggering 4.9 ft per second, a movement so fast that the bug seems almost to have vanished into thin air. This trick helps the jumping moss bug escape predators.

This species and its close cousins represent one of the oldest parts of the Hemiptera group. Moss bugs lived on Earth before the break up of the world's continents, 180 million years ago.

LENGTH: .12 in.
FOUND IN: Eastern Australia
DIET: Moss

CHILEAN MOSS BUG
(Peloridium pomponorum)

Peloridium pomponorum was discovered in 2014 by a team of intrepid insect scientists. Like many moss bugs, it possesses wings so tiny that it cannot fly. Subsequent research trips may locate some individuals of this species that have true wings.

Recent research has shown that male Chilean moss bugs can communicate with females by vibrating their abdomens to make a low humming noise. This noise may help females decide whether or not a male would make a suitable father for her offspring.

LENGTH: .13–.16 in.
FOUND IN: Rainforests of Chile
DIET: Sphagnum mosses

COTTONY CUSHION SCALE

(Icerya purchasi)

The cottony cushion scale is unusual among scale insects for its ability to move around throughout its life. As a nymph, this species can easily move from branch to branch and even travels through the air in high winds to colonize other trees and shrubs. When feeding, the insect's cushionlike covering offers protection from predators.

Most individuals of this species are both male and female at once. Although some are born completely male, no one has ever found a true female of this scale insect.

LENGTH: .27–.35 in.

DIET: Many varieties of woody plants

FOUND IN: Originally found in Australasia; now spread worldwide

PINEAPPLE MEALYBUG

(Dysmicoccus brevipes)

Through its insatiable appetite, the pineapple mealybug can destroy whole plantations of pineapple trees. This makes them a serious pest. Pineapple trees can also suffer extra damage through a species of fungus that eats their honeydew, created by the mealybug.

Unusually for scale insects, the eggs of the pineapple mealybug hatch within her body and she gives "birth" to her nymphs all at once when conditions are just right. This means she can protect her young nymphs from insects that might eat her eggs.

LENGTH: Up to .08 in.

DIET: Sap from pineapple trees

FOUND IN: Originated in Central and South America; now found worldwide in pineapple plantations

SOCIAL BEES (HYMENOPTERA)

Bees are close relatives of wasps and ants. Together these insects form a group called the "Hymenoptera." Of the 16,000 known bee species, many form complex colonies, often ruled over by a noticeably larger queen. These are the social bees.

WESTERN HONEY BEE

(Apis mellifera)

The western honey bee is a master of complex communication. When worker bees return to their nest, they perform a special bottom-waggling dance to their coworkers. The amount of vertical and horizontal waggling tells other colony-mates of the direction and distance of suitable flowers from which nectar can be gathered. This is one of the most incredible acts of communication in the insect world.

This bee species stores in its nest sugars gathered from nectar and adds special ingredients that guard this special liquid from attack by fungi and bacteria—this is honey. Honey is an important source of food for humans, which has led, over many thousands of years, to the western honey bee becoming one of the only insects to be domesticated by humans. Today, these hardworking bees provide an important service to farmers, pollinating their crops and providing us with delicious honey. Each year, it is thought that the western honey bee contributes between $15 billion and $20 billion dollars to the world's economy.

LENGTH: Workers .4–.6 in.; queens .7–.8 in.

DIET: Nectar

FOUND IN: Every continent on Earth except Antarctica

BUFF-TAILED BUMBLEBEE

(Bombus terrestris)

The queen buff-tailed bumblebee rarely leaves her nest. Instead, she spends all of her energy laying eggs. These unfertilized eggs hatch into female worker bees, which leave the nest and forage for nectar from flowers. Workers are quick learners. They learn to associate specific colors of flower with the most sugar-rich nectar.

Later in the year, the buff-tailed bumblebee produces a batch of male bees called drones. These will pair off with other queen buff-tailed bumblebees to make a new nest.

LENGTH: Workers .4–.7 in.; queens .8–.87 in.

DIET: Nectar from flowers

FOUND IN: Originally found throughout Europe; now an invasive species in some countries after accidental release

PATAGONIAN BUMBLEBEE

(Bombus dahlbomii)

With its fluffy body and monstrous size, the Patagonian bumblebee is often called the "flying mouse." This species is a giant among bumblebees—almost double the size of most other species.

While most bumblebee workers frequently move from place to place when seeking nectar, the large size of the Patagonian bumblebee means that workers spend more time walking or flying from flower to flower upon a single food plant. This saves vital energy and reduces the bee's chances of being blown about by high winds.

LENGTH: Workers up to .75 in.; queens up to 1.57 in.

FOUND IN: Temperate forests of southern South America

DIET: Nectar from flowers

SOLITARY BEES (HYMENOPTERA)

Rather than live in a nest busy with workers, many bees live a solitary life. Females lay eggs in special chambers and young are cared for and reared into adulthood, when they will fly from the nest to mate and have babies of their own.

WALLACE'S GIANT BEE
(Megachile pluto)

For many years, Wallace's giant bee was presumed to be extinct. Then, in 2019, scientists observed and filmed one flying in the wild rainforests of Indonesia. This is thought to be the largest bee species in the world—females have a body as long as an adult human thumb.

Wallace's giant bee is part of a family known as resin bees. Resin bees make underground nests that are held together with balls of sticky tree resin. Wallace's giant bee makes its resin nests within the nest of another insect species, the termite.

LENGTH: Females up to 1.5 in.; males .9 in.

FOUND IN: Known from the Indonesian islands of Bacan, Halmahera, and Tidore

DIET: Nectar and plant resin

ALFALFA LEAFCUTTER BEE
(Megachile rotundata)

Female leafcutter bees are well-known for their habit of biting little circles out of leaves and then carrying them back to their nests. With these plant cuttings, the female creates a thimble-shaped cell in a rotting log or similar habitat in which her baby grub will grow, fed by pollen and nectar.

Because the alfalfa leafcutter bee is a very skilled pollinator of fruits and vegetables, including carrots, farmers have transported these bees throughout the world to help them raise bumper crops.

LENGTH: .24–.35 in.

FOUND IN: Once a European species, but now found on all continents except Antarctica

DIET: Nectar and pollen from a variety of plants

NEON CUCKOO BEE
(Thyreus nitidulus)

The neon cuckoo bee is a nest parasite. Females seek out the nests of a related bee species and, when the coast is clear, will enter and lay a secret egg of their own. The grub that hatches from this egg will eat the food left for the other bee grubs and sometimes eat the grubs as well.

This cuckoolike behavior is not unique to the neon cuckoo bee. In all, several thousand bee species have taken up parasitic behavior like this, making it a very common way for some bees to successfully raise offspring.

LENGTH: .5–.6 in.

DIET: Nectar and pollen

FOUND IN: Throughout Australia, Indonesia, and Southeast Asia

DILEMMA ORCHID BEE
(Euglossa dilemma)

To impress nearby females, the male dilemma orchid bee has to collect a variety of ingredients with which he concocts his own brand of perfume. As well as gathering fragrant tree juices and herbs, he also visits a special kind of orchid known for its unusual smell, storing the ingredients in a special pit on his hind legs. When his fragrance is ready, he visits nearby female orchid bees and flaps his wings vigorously so that the scent wafts her way.

LENGTH: Approximately .5 in.

DIET: Nectar

FOUND IN: Throughout Central America

PARASITE WASPS (HYMENOPTERA)

All female hymenopterans have a special tube (called an ovipositor) through which eggs can be squirted into hard-to-reach places. While many wasps lay their eggs into tree bark or soil using their ovipositor, thousands of wasp species opt for somewhere else to lay their eggs—the bodies of other insects and their larvae.

EMERALD COCKROACH WASP
(Ampulex compressa)

The female emerald cockroach wasp watches for cockroaches, especially nice plump ones. When she spots one, she approaches. Using her ovipositor, she carefully stings the cockroach in a specific part of its brain, which stops it from being able to walk of its own accord. It effectively becomes a mindless zombie, which the wasp can treat as her slave.

Gripping the cockroach's antennae with her powerful jaws, the emerald cockroach wasp then gently pulls her prey back to her nest as if it were a dog on a leash. There, she lays a single egg on its underside from which a cockroach-eating grub will emerge. This grub eats the cockroach alive while the female emerald cockroach wasp goes off to search for other cockroaches to brainwash with her ghoulish behavior.

No other animal group on Earth has mastered such an advanced form of parasitism. Although it sounds monstrous, the actions of parasitic wasps like this one help keep pests at bay.

LENGTH: .87 in.

DIET: Cockroaches

FOUND IN: Tropical parts of South Asia, Africa, and the Pacific Islands

GIANT ICHNEUMON WASP

(Megarhyssa macrurus)

To locate grubs tunneling beneath the bark, the female giant ichneumon wasp feels for vibrations deep within the tree using its highly sensitive antennae. When it senses movement below, it drills its giant ovipositor into the bark, penetrating the sleeping chambers of the burrowing grubs and injecting its eggs into their bodies.

The ichneumon larvae that hatch from these tiny eggs will eat the grubs alive. Two weeks later, they will pupate and emerge from the side of the tree as adult wasps… and the whole gruesome cycle begins again.

LENGTH: Up to 5.12 in. including ovipositor

FOUND IN: Eastern parts of the US and into southern Canada

DIET: Grubs

HYPERPARASITIC ICHNEUMON WASP

(Lysibia nana)

When some plants are attacked by caterpillars, they can call for help by releasing a special chemical odor into the air. This attracts parasitic wasps, which attack the caterpillars, laying eggs that will hatch into hungry grubs that eat the caterpillars alive. However, *Lysibia nana* is also interested in this smell. It homes in on the fragrance, seeking out the parasitic wasp grubs, within which it lays its own parasitic eggs. Incredibly, this species is a parasite of a parasite.

This sort of lifestyle (called hyperparasitism) is rare in insects.

LENGTH: Up to .32 in.

DIET: Nectar

FOUND IN: Originally known from Europe and Asia, but now likely to be widespread across the world

TINY WASPS (HYMENOPTERA)

PARASITIC FIG WASP
(Apocrypta guineensis)

For its size, the parasitic fig wasp has one of the longest ovipositors of any wasp. With a titaniumlike sheath, it can drill into the fruits of fig trees, within which tiny grubs of a different wasp species live.

Because each species of fig tree produces its own type of fruit, fig wasps and their parasites have become adapted to suit a range of fig trees. For this reason, there are more than 900 fig wasp species and hundreds of parasitic wasps that specialize upon them.

LENGTH: .12–.24 in.

FOUND IN: Central belt of Africa

DIET: Nectar

JUMPING GALL WASP
(Neuroterus saltatorius)

When laying their eggs on leaves and stems, many wasp species trick the tree into making a special housing for their baby grub called a gall. Within this comfortable and nutritious gall, the wasp grub develops and eventually leaves the gall as an adult.

Most galls remain in place on the tree, but the galls of the jumping gall wasp regularly fall off the tree and drop to the floor below. By shaking its body violently inside its protective gall, the grub manages to wriggle itself into cracks within the soil so that it can see out the winter months in safety.

LENGTH: .08–.12 in.

FOUND IN: Western US

DIET: Plant juices

KIKIKI FAIRY WASP
(Kikiki huna)

The Kikiki fairy wasp is the world's smallest known flying insect. The species is so tiny it could quite happily perch on the head of a pin. Being tiny helps the Kikiki fairy wasp, for this species seeks out tiny eggs of other insects—including beetles, dragonflies and cicadas—and lays its eggs within them.

The Kikiki fairy wasp is one of around 1,400 known fairy wasp species, but there are likely to be many thousands more that scientists have not yet spotted.

LENGTH: .005–.008 in. — you could fit five in a single full-stop

FOUND IN: Known from Hawai'i, Costa Rica, and Trinidad

DIET: Not yet known

FAIRYFLY
(Gonatocerus ashmeadi)

This tiny wasp is used as a weapon to destroy a pest called the glassy winged sharpshooter, an invasive insect species that damages crops.

Because this tiny wasp injects its hungry grubs into the eggs of this pest, scientists release thousands of these fairyflies into affected areas where they go to work seeking out and killing the eggs. This is one of many ways in which insects can be used to help keep crops safe from pests.

LENGTH: Approximately .04 in.

FOUND IN: Throughout southern regions of the US

DIET: Insect eggs

SOCIAL WASPS (HYMENOPTERA)

Social wasps are among the most coordinated and charismatic of invertebrates. Like social bees, their nests are ruled by a single egg-laying queen tended to by thousands—or sometimes tens of thousands—of workers. In terms of numbers alone, they rank as one of the world's most numerous insect species.

ASIAN GIANT HORNET
(Vespa mandarinia)

The Asian giant hornet is the only wasp known to leave scent trails upon food items, directing others within the colony to new sources of food. They are also able to communicate with one another by licking nest-mates or, when threatened, by clacking their jaws noisily.

As well as eating beetles and mantises, the Asian giant hornet often attacks the nests of other wasps and bees. So adept at hunting is this species, that a squadron of only 50 hornets is all it takes to bring down an entire colony of bees.

LENGTH: Queens up to 2 in.; workers commonly 1.4–1.6 in.

DIET: Other insects, particularly bees and wasps

FOUND IN: Temperate and tropical parts of eastern Asia

PAPER WASP
(Polybia emaciata)

For millions of years, a group of social wasps have chewed up wood fibers and mixed this with saliva to make paper for their nests. These are the so-called paper wasps. *Polybia emaciata* differs from other paper wasps in that its nests are made from specially collected mud that dries like cement.

Polybia emaciata has another unusual characteristic. Its nests contain not one but many queens. These nests stay together because the queens are all closely related to one another, meaning they rule the nests as a close-knit family.

LENGTH: Approximately .3–.4 in.

FOUND IN: Mainly found in South America

DIET: Flies, beetles, and nectar

COMMON WASP
(Vespula vulgaris)

Though many people consider this inquisitive wasp a pest of picnics and barbeques, the truth is that the common wasp performs an important pest control service that we would miss if it were to disappear.

For each 10,000 sq ft of countryside, this species is likely to remove 176 lbs of invertebrate prey, including spiders. In Britain alone, wasps recycle 15,000 tons of insects each year.

Common wasps become most of a nuisance to humans in late summer, when their nests collapse and the queen dies, leaving her workers homeless and hungry.

LENGTH: Workers .47–.67 in.; queens nearer .8 in.

FOUND IN: A variety of habitats across Europe and Asia

DIET: Mostly nectar and invertebrates

MEXICAN HONEY WASP
(Brachygastra mellifica)

The Mexican honey wasp performs a range of services for humans. Firstly, it is one of the only wasp species known to make honey, a liquid storage solution for nutritious sugars. This delicious honey is eaten all year round. The larvae are also considered a delicacy by local people.

The Mexican honey wasp also provides an important pollination service. Long before the introduction of the western honey bee, it was the Mexican honey wasp that pollinated many of the flowers that exist in Central and South America, including those of the avocado tree.

LENGTH: .27–.35 in.

FOUND IN: Throughout subtropical regions of North and South America

DIET: Insects and nectar

SAWFLIES (HYMENOPTERA)

Unlike wasps, sawflies do not have a defined "wasp-waist" between their abdomen and thorax. Their name comes from their sawlike ovipositor used to cut into plants where their eggs are laid. Around 8,000 sawfly species are known, although more are discovered each year.

SIREX WOODWASP
(Sirex noctilio)

When searching for a suitable place to lay her eggs, the sirex woodwasp homes in on the telltale odors of a dying tree. While laying her eggs in the bark, she introduces a small amount of a special fungus that digests dead trees. As it grows, this fungus forms the main diet of the tiny grubs that hatch from her eggs.

Sadly, this fungus can go on to kill some trees, making the sirex woodwasp a pest species in many parts of the world.

LENGTH: .35–1.42 in.

DIET: Pollen and nectar

FOUND IN: Native to North Africa, Europe, and Asia

GREATER HORNTAIL
(Urocerus gigas)

With its chunky body and repeating bands of black and yellow, the greater horntail does all it can to look like a venomous wasp. In fact, it is harmless. The species lays its eggs in trees, favoring pine trees. Its grubs live within these trees for up to five years.

By investigating and copying the sawlike ovipositor of horntails, engineers have begun to invent microscopic drills that can cut with greater flexibility and precision. These tiny tools may one day be used in human surgery.

LENGTH: .4–1.6 in.

DIET: Pollen and nectar

FOUND IN: Parts of Northern Africa, and across Europe and Asia.

PARASITIC WOODWASP
(Orussus terminalis)

The sawflies evolved 200 million years ago in the age of the first dinosaurs. Fossils suggest that in those days, most sawflies were parasites of other insects, injecting their eggs into their bodies in the same way that many parasitic wasps do today.

Only a small group of parasitic sawflies live today, many specializing on the wood-dwelling larvae of beetles and other sawflies. They tap their antennae against branches, using their legs to feel for vibrations reflected from hidden larvae deep underneath the bark. This is the sawfly version of a bat's echolocation.

LENGTH: Approximately .51 in.

DIET: Likely to feed on nectar and pollen

FOUND IN: North America

GREEN SAWFLY
(Rhogogaster viridis)

The larvae of the green sawfly are voracious eaters, capable of stripping whole shrubs bare within days. Although their larvae look like caterpillars, sawfly larvae only possess a single pair of tiny eyes. Butterfly and moth caterpillars, on the other hand, have many pairs of eyes.

As with many hymenopterans, the adult green sawfly has two large eyes on the front of its head, with three smaller eyes (called ocelli) on the top of the head. The function of these small eyes is a subject of great debate among insect scientists.

LENGTH: Up to .6 in.

DIET: Nectar and small insects

FOUND IN: Primarily throughout meadows and woodlands of Europe

ANTS (HYMENOPTERA)

Ants evolved from wasplike ancestors at the end of the age of the dinosaurs, and today represent one of the most successful parts of the insect group. Many ants are social, consisting of societies ruled by queens responsible for egg-laying. There may be as many as 22,000 different ant species on Earth.

TASMANIAN INCHMAN
(Myrmecia esuriens)

The Tasmanian inchman is known for its extremely aggressive nature and its painful sting. It defends its colony with extreme force and, for this reason, most predators leave it alone.

The Tasmanian inchman is unique among ants for having queens that are wingless. Normally, ant colonies have distinct times when fleets of winged queens fly from the nest to found new colonies, but in the case of the Tasmanian inchman, the young queens must clamber through the undergrowth in search of new places to nest.

LENGTH: Queens up to .94 in.; workers up to .71 in.

FOUND IN: Found in Tasmania underneath rocks and fallen trees

DIET: Fruits, seeds, and dead and dying animals

GLIDING ANT
(Cephalotes atratus)

The gliding ant can sail through the air. If knocked off a branch, it swivels its oddly shaped head while falling, swerving back toward the tree's trunk where it lands safely. Many ant species have since been discovered to perform this trick.

Cephalotes atratus can also use its large head to defend the nest from attack by invading army ants. When threatened, hundreds of gliding ants can unite their heads to create a living shield that blocks the nest entrance.

LENGTH: Workers up to .55 in.; queens up to .79 in.

FOUND IN: Lowland tropical rainforests of South America

DIET: Omnivorous; often seen drinking honeydew from aphids

HONEYPOT ANT
(Myrmecocystus mexicanus)

Just as some bees use honey to store sugars in the nest for hard times, some ants also store food up for later. In species of honeypot ants, special workers climb up the walls of the nest and hang from the ceiling. Here, these workers begin to swell up with liquid food, becoming so swollen they become totally immobile. Many honeypot ants are swollen to four or five times their normal size.

In this form, the honeypot ants becoming living food stores for the colony. They can be drained by other workers during times of famine.

LENGTH: Workers up to .28 in.; queens up to .35 in.

FOUND IN: Throughout Mexico and into southwestern states of the US

DIET: Nectar and sugary galls made by plants

LEAFCUTTER ANT
(Atta cephalotes)

The leafcutter ants are one of Earth's oldest farmers. Their colony workers spend their days biting chunks off leaves which are taken back to the nest where they are used to grow a special fungus which their larvae require to grow.

The nests of this leafcutter ant species are among the most carefully constructed of all ant nests. They are often situated on open areas of forest, so that gusts of wind can ensure the nest doesn't get too hot. These nests also have within them a garbage dump where dead colony-mates are buried.

LENGTH: Workers up to .55 in.; queens up to .87 in.

FOUND IN: Throughout tropical regions of South America

DIET: Leaves and leaf fungus

ARMY ANTS AND SLAVE-MAKERS (HYMENOPTERA)

About 200 ant species have taken up a nomadic existence. They roam jungles and grasslands in great troupes, often carrying their nest (including egg-laying queens and larvae) as they go. These are the army ants. Army ants are among the most aggressive of all ant species.

ECITON ARMY ANT
(Eciton burchellii)

When establishing a new territory, Eciton army ants create a protective shelter for the queen and her larvae, made from thousands of interlocking worker ants. This so-called bivouac acts like a living wall, which can be opened and closed to let air in and out of the colony and keep the larvae at the right temperature. While the young are tended to, other worker ants go on raids to find food.

Eciton army ant raids are one of nature's most deadly phenomena. In all, 200,000 worker ants go on the rampage, raiding and capturing insects and carrying their dead bodies back to the nest. The raids are frequently carried out on wasp nests, devouring and eating the wasps and their grubs. The area covered by the raiding ants can be 65 ft wide and 660 ft long.

Once a local area has been exploited thoroughly by the Eciton army ant, they prepare to move their bivouac to an area not yet explored.

LENGTH: .12–.47 in.

FOUND IN: Tropical jungles of Central and South America

DIET: Invertebrates, small frogs, lizards, and dead birds

DRIVER ANT
(Dorylus gribodoi)

When food becomes scarce, driver ants move across the land in columns, 50 million strong. These vast armies consume everything in their path.

Some members of the driver ant colony are larger than normal workers and possess wide and powerful jaws. These are the soldiers, a specific form (or "caste") of driver ant that makes sure the group is kept safe.

Though many people fear this species of driver ant, some local communities celebrate their arrival because these ants kill off many of the pests that affect farmers and their livestock.

LENGTH: Workers .03–.11 in.

FOUND IN: Rainforests and savannas across western Africa

DIET: Invertebrates and small amphibians, reptiles and birds

SLAVE-MAKING ANT
(Polyergus lucidus)

Some ant species have evolved to take out and capture the workers of neighboring ant species, using them for their own requirements. These ants are called "slave-makers" or, to use the scientific term, "brood parasites."

Polyergus lucidus is totally dependent on other ants for its survival. For a colony to live, it captures larvae from other ant nests and raises them as if they were their own. These larvae grow up to become workers, hunting for *Polyergus lucidus* as if they were part of the family.

LENGTH: Workers .22–.28 in.

FOUND IN: Prairies, pastures, and fields in eastern parts of the US

DIET: Omnivorous

TINY ANTS (HYMENOPTERA)

Some of the most incredible and successful ants on Earth are also the smallest ant species. What they lack in size, they more than make up for in coordination and determination.

THIEF ANT
(Solenopsis molesta)

Some thief ant workers are so small they can barely be seen with the human eye. They set up their colonies near the nests of other ant species and sneak in to grab supplies that they carry back to their own nest.

Thief ants also steal from humans. Because of their tiny size, thief ants often go unnoticed. They can live in houses for years, stealing tiny amounts of food from kitchen floors and cupboards. They are also attracted to grease, hence their other nickname—the grease ant.

LENGTH: .02–.12 in.

FOUND IN: Native to many parts of North America

DIET: Sugary foods and the larvae of other ant species

PHARAOH ANT
(Monomorium pharaonis)

The pharaoh ant is one of the world's most traveled ants. No one is sure where this tropical ant originally came from, but today it thrives in places with central heating, including hospitals, schools, and homes.

The secret of the pharaoh ant's success is that, where most ant colonies have a single queen, pharaoh ants have multiple queens. This means that colonies regularly split up to found new colonies elsewhere. The fact that they spread quickly makes eradicating this species from buildings very difficult.

LENGTH: Workers .06–.08 in.; queens .14–.2 in.

FOUND IN: Throughout the world in warm, human habitations

DIET: Omnivorous

TWISTED-WINGED INSECTS (STREPSIPTERA)

The twisted-winged insects are a mysterious part of the insect family that were for many centuries completely overlooked. Females of these insects are parasites that live upon and within the abdomens of other insects.

STYLOPS MELITTAE

This twisted-winged insect begins life as a highly mobile larva that waits upon flower blossoms to climb aboard sand bees when they visit to drink nectar. In the coming days and weeks, the larva moves around on the bee's back, drinking its internal fluids before wedging its head into the bee's body and turning into a pupa.

After pupating, most adult *Stylops melittae* are females. Females live their whole lives with their heads poking out of the bee's abdomen, awaiting the arrival of tiny males with which they mate and produce more tiny larvae.

LENGTH: Adults up to .08 in.

FOUND IN: Throughout Europe

DIET: Females drink body fluids from insect hosts

XENOS VESPARUM

When an adult paper wasp becomes infected with an adult *Xenos vesparum*, the tiny parasite manipulates the brain of the paper wasp, causing the wasp to seek out other wasps. This is the parasite's way of finding others of its kind.

If a wasp infected with a male *Xenos vesparum* meets a wasp infected with a female *Xenos vesparum*, the male tears itself from its host, killing the paper wasp in the process, and climbs aboard the other paper wasp to mate and have babies with the female.

LENGTH: Up to .12 in.

FOUND IN: Throughout North America

DIET: Female drinks body fluids from insect hosts

WATER BEETLES (COLEOPTERA)

With about 400,000 known species, the order of beetles (Coleoptera) is the largest part of the insect group. Beetles account for 40% of all insects and 25% of all known animal species. Water beetles are one dynamic and successful part of the group—around 2,000 water beetle species are known.

COMMON WHIRLIGIG BEETLE
(Gyrinus natator)

The common whirligig beetle spends most of its life skating on the surface of lakes and ponds. In a rare example of insect echolocation, this species sends waves of vibrations out over the water's surface and feels for the ripples from these waves as they reflect off nearby objects. Its eyes are split across the middle, so that it can see both above and below the water.

Like nearly all beetles, whirligig beetles occasionally fly. High up in the air, they scan the ground for signs of new water bodies to colonize.

LENGTH: Up to .24 in.

FOUND IN: Freshwater across Europe and Asia

DIET: Small crustaceans and insects dying on the water surface

GREAT DIVING BEETLE
(Dytiscus marginalis)

The great diving beetle is the great white shark of water beetles. Once an adult finds its way to a pond, it begins chasing after tadpoles, young fish, and other water beetles, altering whole communities in the process. Once the pond is empty of prey, the great diving beetle cleans its eyes and wings before taking to the air once more.

Unusually for beetles, the larva of a great diving beetle is as predatory as the adult. They regularly attack and overpower small fish and amphibians.

LENGTH: Larvae up to 2.36 in.; adults up to 1.4 in.

FOUND IN: Europe and northern parts of Asia

DIET: Water invertebrates, tadpoles, and fish

MEGADYTES DUCALIS

Only one single specimen of this enormous Brazilian diving beetle has ever been collected. It was found in the 1800s from an unknown part of Brazil, reportedly in a puddle of water at the bottom of a canoe.

This is likely to be the largest water beetle in the world and so many scientists have tried to discover whether it still lives today. Because no specimens have been collected in more than 100 years, most scientists suspect that the Brazilian diving beetle is likely to be extinct.

LENGTH: 1.87 in.

DIET: Likely to include invertebrates and small fish

FOUND IN: Remote Amazonian regions of Brazil

AUSTRALIAN SUBTERRANEAN WATER BEETLE

(Limbodessus bennetti)

Most water beetles are terrestrial insects that have become adapted for life under the surface. The Australian subterranean water beetle is unusual, however, because it has adapted from living on land to a particular digging way of life. This species spends its day working through wet soil at the water's edge in search of prey.

The Australian subterranean water beetle is known to live in a small patch of dry and remote outback in Australia. As far as we know, the world's entire population of this beetle lives in a single pond.

LENGTH: .06 in.

DIET: Other invertebrates

FOUND IN: The Pilbara region of western Australia

GROUND BEETLES (COLEOPTERA)

Beetles are known for their armored wing cases known as elytra. In the ground beetles, these elytra have lots of ridges along them. Ground beetles are also known for producing toxic secretions that come from glands on their abdomens. In all, 40,000 ground beetle species have been discovered.

GOLDEN GROUND BEETLE

(Carabus auratus)

Rather than using its toxic secretions to scare away predators, the golden ground beetle uses them to help it swallow food. Once it catches snails, insects, and worms, it pins them down with its jaws and sprays special chemicals that melt its prey, helping its meal become easier to digest.

Like other large ground beetles, the golden ground beetle has elytra that are fused together. This means that, unlike the vast majority of beetles, this species cannot fly.

LENGTH: .67–.79 in.

DIET: Ground-dwelling invertebrates

FOUND IN: Fields and shrublands throughout central and western parts of Europe

VIOLIN BEETLE

(Mormolyce phyllodes)

The violin beetle camouflages almost perfectly among the fallen leaves of the forest floor. As well as helping this ground beetle hide, its wide and incredibly thin elytra help it to get in the cracks between clumps of soil or under bark where its prey is most easily found.

If threatened, the violin beetle can spray a chemical that many mammals find disgusting. This chemical, known as butyric acid, is said to smell like a mixture of sweat and butter.

LENGTH: 2.36–3.94 in.

DIET: Insect larvae

FOUND IN: The rainforests of Southeast Asia

BOMBARDIER ANT'S GUEST BEETLE
(Cerapterus lacerates)

This ground beetle is a master of disguise. It lives its life within the busy nests of ants and manages to blend in through the use of special chemicals that make it smell like a friendly worker ant. Scientists think that this beetle can also make a special sound that mimics that of the queen ant, meaning that ants actively seek to keep it safe.

Like others of its close family, the bombardier ant's guest beetle is capable of squirting two special chemicals at once. When mixed, these chemicals create a sizzling reaction that burns the skin of potential predators.

LENGTH: .39–.47 in.

DIET: Ant eggs and larvae

FOUND IN: Among ant nests of southern Africa

FESTIVE TIGER BEETLE
(Cicindela scutellaris)

The festive tiger beetle is one of the fastest beetles on land, capable of sprinting over hot sand and soil in pursuit of other insects, which it pulls apart with incredibly strong jaws. In a single second, these beetles and their close relatives can scuttle more than 3 ft across the floor.

Like many ground beetles, the larvae of tiger beetles are also endowed with adaptations for killing. Their wormlike larvae have a trapdoorlike head that flips backward when passing insects step too close. Caught offguard, the unfortunate prey then tumbles helplessly into the larva's monster jaws.

LENGTH: .43–.51 in.

DIET: Other insects

FOUND IN: Often found on sandy or clay soils near water; widespread across eastern parts of North America

ROVE BEETLES (COLEOPTERA)

The rove beetles are the largest known family of beetles, with 63,000 species known from habitats all over the world. The secret of the rove beetle's success is their incredibly flexible abdomen, which can be used in self-defense or for squeezing into small and hard-to-reach places.

DEVIL'S COACH HORSE BEETLE
(Ocypus olens)

When threatened by predators, the devil's coach horse rears up its tail like a scorpion ready to strike. It also holds its jaws wide open to inform approaching animals of its powerful bite.

It takes its name from the strange oozing liquid that can be produced from its abdomen. This stinky fluid was, in medieval times, thought to be the work of the devil.

The devil's coach horse is one of the world's most familiar rove beetles.

LENGTH: .79–1.18 in.

DIET: Nocturnal predator of worms, snails, spiders, and woodlice

FOUND IN: Damp meadows and woodlands throughout Europe and North Africa

PICTURED ROVE BEETLE
(Thinopinus pictus)

In the depths of night, the pictured rove beetle leaves its sandy burrow to find food. It crawls toward the parts of the beach where seaweeds and other detritus are washed up from the high tide, and squeezes its body underneath the vegetation in search of jumping crustaceans called beach-hoppers. Around the world, about 400 rove beetle species have taken on this way of life, conquering an unpredictable seaside habitat where few other animals manage to survive.

LENGTH: .67–.71 in.

DIET: Beach hoppers, flies, and sea slaters

FOUND IN: Sandy beaches on the West Coast of the US

ARMY ANT ROVE BEETLE
(Ecitophya simulans)

As the army ants of South America make their way through the undergrowth, they have among them a stowaway—a rove beetle that sneaks around feeding on scraps without any of the ants ever noticing. To permit this secretive way of life, the army ant rove beetle has evolved a body shape very similar to that of an army ant. But because many ants are blind, the army ant rove beetle has also evolved to smell and taste like a friendly ant as well.

LENGTH: .12–.47 in.

FOUND IN: Rainforests of South America

DIET: Scraps left by ants

HAIRY ROVE BEETLE
(Creophilus maxillosus)

The hairy rove beetle is drawn to the smell of rotting animals. When it discovers a corpse, it forces its way into the body of the dead animal to feed on the tiny animals within that are involved in decomposition, particularly maggots, which they carry into the undergrowth to devour.

As with many other rove beetles, this species produces chemicals from the tip of its tail that other animals find disgusting. The hairy rove beetle's toxic surprise is especially good at scaring away ants.

LENGTH: .47–.71 in.

FOUND IN: Eastern parts of the US

DIET: Insects and their larvae

SCARABS (COLEOPTERA)

The scarabs are a family of armored beetles, many of which are excellent diggers. Because of their incredible colors and unusual behaviors, many human cultures celebrate some scarab species. In total, scientists have discovered more than 30,000 species.

SACRED SCARAB
(Scarabaeus sacer)

The sacred scarab performs an important dung-removal service. Using powerful legs, it rolls the droppings of mammals into a special underground den where it spends days eating in secret, away from predators. When breeding, the female sacred scarab makes a much larger dung ball in which she places a single egg. This grub will eat the dung ball before pupating.

The sacred scarab was an important symbol for the ancient Egyptians. They saw the way this species rolls balls of dung and it reminded them of the way the sun was thought to roll through the sky.

LENGTH: Approximately .4 in.

DIET: Animal droppings

FOUND IN: Coastal dunes and marshes across northern Africa, southern Europe, and parts of Asia

GOLIATH BEETLE
(Goliathus goliatus)

In terms of its bulk, the goliath beetle and its close relatives are among the largest insects on the planet. Full-grown adults are the size of a human hand and weigh more than twice the weight of a mouse. Incredibly, this species of goliath beetle is an impressive flier. It uses long wings, which are folded underneath its elytra.

The male goliath beetle is armed and prepared for battle. A two-pronged horn on its head can be used to duel, shove, and topple over rivals attempting to muscle in on nearby females.

LENGTH: 1.97–4.33 in.

DIET: Tree sap and fruit

FOUND IN: Africa's tropical rainforests

EASTERN HERCULES BEETLE
(Dynastes tityus)

The large horn on the head of the eastern Hercules beetle shows off to others how big and strong he is. The horns of these so-called rhinoceros beetles are largest in males that have found the best trees in which to feed.

Adult eastern Hercules beetles only live for a matter of months, often dying soon after they have laid their eggs. These eggs hatch into grubs which live within rotting trees eating dead wood. Like many scarabs, the C-shaped grubs often live for a year or more, and perform an important job clearing the forest of dead wood.

LENGTH: 1.57–2.36 in.

DIET: Tree sap

FOUND IN: Eastern and southeastern parts of the US

WHITE SCARAB BEETLE
(Cyphochilus insulanus)

To camouflage among mushrooms, the white scarab beetle has hit upon a unique trick. Though its exoskeleton is black like other scarabs, it is covered in microscopic scales that scatter light in such a way that all of the colors in light are reflected evenly—this creates a pure white color unlike anything else in nature.

The whiteness of this insect has even attracted the interest of scientists who want to investigate whether this color can be artificially created for use in human technology, such as in white paper, fabrics, and paint.

LENGTH: .98–1.2 in.

DIET: Leaves

FOUND IN: Rainforests of Southeast Asia

STAG AND CLOWN BEETLES (COLEOPTERA)

Many beetle families are named for their curious adaptations. Stag beetles are so-named for the male's giant jaws, which resemble the antlers of a deer stag. Clown beetles take their name from their frequent habit of trying to fool predators by playing dead.

STAG BEETLE
(Lucanus cervus)

The imposing "antlers" of the male stag beetle are used during the mating season, when males face off against other males to battle for females. Occasionally, male stag beetles also duel over food, including tree sap and decaying fruit.

Their jaws are so wide they cannot be used to bite predators, so male stag beetles have few defenses if approached. Most will attempt to escape by flying away. The female, on the other hand, is capable of delivering a painful bite if disturbed.

LENGTH: Females up to 2.36 in.; males up to 3.54 in.

FOUND IN: Woodlands throughout Europe

DIET: Sugary plant fluids and decaying fruit

GOLDEN STAG BEETLE
(Lamprima aurata)

The golden stag beetle comes in a range of colors that differ from place to place. These different colored beetles are called morphs. In some parts of Australia, golden stag beetle morphs are bright green and golden, and in other parts they are bronze or dark purple. No one knows for sure why these differences in color occur between individuals in some insects. Some scientists think it could be to do with special chemicals found in different species of trees that young grubs eat while they are young.

LENGTH: .55–1.26 in.

FOUND IN: Throughout Australia

DIET: Dead wood including eucalyptus trees

POULTRYHOUSE PILL BEETLE
(Carcinops pumilio)

In a single day, a poultryhouse pill beetle can eat more than 100 fly eggs and maggots, which it tears apart with powerful hooked mouthparts. For this reason, the species is often found near smelly piles of bird and bat droppings and near the bodies of dead animals.

Its fondness for houseflies makes the poultryhouse pill beetle a very important pest controller, particularly in chicken coops where they are used by farmers to keep down the number of flies buzzing around.

LENGTH: .06–.1 in.

DIET: Fly eggs and larvae

FOUND IN: Originally known from Africa, Europe, and Asia; now worldwide

UNICOLOROUS CLOWN BEETLE
(Hister unicolor)

Few scientists ever get to see the unicolorous clown beetle for real. This is because it spends most of its life hiding within animal droppings. Even when a specimen is uncovered, this species can be almost impossible to see. It plays dead by pulling its legs against its body and becoming statue-still—a trick that makes it harder for predators to spot them.

Rather than feeding upon droppings like some other beetle species, the unicolorous clown beetle feeds on the larvae of manure-eating flies. Like many clown beetles, it performs an important pest-control service.

LENGTH: .3–.4 in.

DIET: Insect eggs and larvae

FOUND IN: Throughout Europe

JEWEL BEETLES (COLEOPTERA)

The jewel beetles are named for their beautiful colors, which sparkle and shimmer in sunlight. Their young are known as flat-headed borers, for their habit of drilling through trees while munching on wood. In all, 15,500 species of jewel beetle have been discovered by scientists—most species are so secretive that they do not have a common name.

TEMOGNATHA ALTERNATA

This strikingly colored jewel beetle was first discovered in 1882, but its secretive nature makes it very hard for scientists to study. So mysterious is this species that no one has yet seen or studied its larvae or eggs.

Like other jewel beetles, it may be that *Temognatha alternata* seeks out wood that has been damaged by forest fires to lay its eggs. To find the most suitable wood for its young, some jewel beetles can sense the smoke from forest fires from up to 50 miles away.

LENGTH: Up to 1.03 in.

FOUND IN: Forests of Queensland, Australia

DIET: Unknown

GOLDEN BUPRESTID
(Buprestis aurulenta)

This beetle spends many years of its life as a burrowing larva within conifer trees. The submerged tunnels that these larvae create (called mines) can damage the bark of the tree, causing problems for tree plantation owners who want to cut down trees and use the wood for building houses.

To test if a potential tree is home to larvae of this jewel beetle species, some experts carefully put their ear to the bark to listen for the sound of their munching.

LENGTH: Adults .59 in.

DIET: Adults feed on leaves and wood

FOUND IN: Native to western parts of North America

CHRYSOCHROA FULGIDISSIMA

When looked at from different angles, this stunning jewel beetle appears to change color. From some sides, it looks purple; from others, blue; from other angles, it is red or pink. Japanese people refer to this jewel beetle as "tamamushi"—a word used to describe people who make statements that can be read in many different ways.

The beetle's iridescent colors are produced through layers of tiny microscopic structures that split light into a rainbow of colors that are reflected in lots of different directions at once. This is the same colorful effect seen on the underside of DVDs and CDs.

In some beetles, unusual colors like these are thought to be produced by coincidence—the tiny ridges on elytra that help beetles deflect water or mud just happen to produce rainbow colors. However, in *Chrysochroa fulgidissima*, the colorings are so dynamic and eye-catching that they are likely to be used by males and females to catch one another's attention as they move through the forest.

LENGTH: Adults 1.2–1.6 in.

FOUND IN: Woodlands and forests of Japan and Korea

DIET: Leaves

FIREFLIES (COLEOPTERA)

The soft-bodied beetles known for creating a ghostly glow from parts of their abdomen are commonly referred to as "fireflies." Each of the 2,000 firefly species so far discovered produce light by creating and mixing special chemicals that glow yellow, green, or pale blue when they react together. This is called bioluminescence.

COMMON GLOWWORM
(Lampyris noctiluca)

Europeans call this species the glowworm because its light is produced by females that are long and wormlike. At night, males fly high in the sky, looking for the special green glow which she uses to guide them toward her.

In recent years, scientists have seen some populations of glowworms begin to disappear. This may be because streetlights are causing the males to get confused. These males fly toward streetlights expecting them to be eager females and instead end up lost and lonely.

LENGTH: Up to 1 in.

FOUND IN: Grasslands across Europe and Asia

DIET: Snails

ROVER FIREFLY
(Photinus carolinus)

So-called rovers get their name from the male beetle's habit of flying from place to place, while flashing a repeated pattern that females look out for. If interested, a watching female will emit a special glow in return.

When lots of males happen to be flying around on the same night, they coordinate their pulses of light together and then switch off their glow all at once, so that they can more clearly see any signals from interested females in the undergrowth below. This makes for an impressive spectacle, which tourists travel many miles to see.

LENGTH: .3–.5 in.

FOUND IN: The US's Great Smoky Mountains

DIET: Plant pollen and nectar

FEMME FATALE FIREFLY

(Photuris pennsylvanica)

The femme fatale firefly is watching the skies for her prey, the male rover firefly. When she spots its familiar glowing patterns, she lets out a flash of her own which mimics the flashing of a female rover firefly. The male swoops down, eager to begin egg-laying—only to come face-to-face with the biting jaws of this predatory firefly. The species is well-named: "femme fatale" is French for "fatal woman."

By eating other fireflies in this way, the femme fatale firefly can produce a poisonous substance in her body that protects her from predators.

LENGTH: .43–.6 in.

FOUND IN: US and Canada

DIET: Fireflies, snails and worms

AQUATICA LATERALIS

Unlike most other fireflies, the larvae of *Aquatica lateralis* live and hunt underwater. It crawls on submerged water plants or runs along the bottom, protected by poisonous spines which guard it from fish. The larvae of *Aquatica lateralis* are commonly found in water-logged rice-fields, where they live for up to a year or more before pupating in wet mud and becoming the adult form.

Impressively, all life stages of this species are capable of bioluminescence. Even the eggs and the pupae are known to give off an eerie greenish glow.

LENGTH: .25–.42 in.

FOUND IN: Wetlands throughout Russia, Japan and Korea

DIET: Invertebrates including snails

LADYBUG BEETLES (COLEOPTERA)

Ladybug beetles are a family of 6,000 beetles known from all over the world. Many species have familiar patterns of spots on their wing cases and have a strange-looking dome-shaped body with six short legs.

MEXICAN BEAN BEETLE
(Epilachna varivestis)

Most ladybug species give humans a free pest-removal service by feeding upon aphids and scale insects. Yet the Mexican bean beetle is different. It has ditched a predatory way of life and now prefers leaves. It particularly favours the juicy leaves of bean plants, making this species a serious problem for farmers who grow these crops.

To limit the spread of the Mexican bean beetle, scientists have bred and released special parasitic wasps, which seek out the beetle's larvae and kill them, keeping their numbers in check.

LENGTH: .24–.28 in.

FOUND IN: Mexico and eastern parts of the US

DIET: Leaves of numerous bean plant species

SEVEN-SPOT LADYBUG
(Coccinella septempunctata)

The familiar patterns of this species warn birds of the distasteful chemicals that they are able to produce from the joints of their legs. Many individuals will also play dead when attacked by birds, pulling their legs close to their body while remaining completely motionless.

This adaptable ladybug is found throughout Europe and now occurs throughout North America after being released there on purpose by farmers eager to control their aphid infestations. Since its release, the seven-spot ladybug has spread and may be threatening other ladybug species in North America.

LENGTH: .3–.4 in.

FOUND IN: Throughout most of the Northern Hemisphere

DIET: Aphids

SCALE-EATING LADYBUG
(Rhyzobius lophanthae)

The scale-eating ladybug has hit upon a clever strategy to get around the armor of its prey, the scale insect. Being small, its larvae squeeze themselves under the wall-like defenses of the scale insect and, once safely inside, they seek out and eat the scale insect's tiny nymphs.

This is not the only ladybug species with larvae that are impressively adapted to hunt and kill their prey. The same is true of many ladybug species. Larvae that are adapted to hunt in this way are called "campodeiform" larvae.

LENGTH: .07–.12 in.

DIET: Scale insects

FOUND IN: Originally known from Queensland and South Australia; introduced to the US and now known to live in many southern areas

HARLEQUIN LADYBUG
(Harmonia axyridis)

The harlequin ladybug is one of the world's most invasive insect species. Originally released by farmers throughout the world to help them deal with aphids, the adaptable nature of this beetle has seen it spread. This is bad news for native ladybug species, which the harlequin ladybug regularly eats.

The harlequin ladybug gets its name from the fact that it wears lots of masks. Its elytra come in many different patterns. Where some individual harlequins have two spots, others have four, ten or even twenty-two spots. This can make telling harlequin ladybugs from other ladybugs very difficult.

LENGTH: .2–.33 in.

DIET: Aphids and other ladybug species

FOUND IN: Originally known from Asia; now found throughout Europe, Africa, and the Americas

DARKLING BEETLES (COLEOPTERA)

More than 20,000 species belong in a superfamily of beetles called the Tenebrionoidea, which are sometimes referred to as darkling beetles. The name "darkling" refers to the fact that many species like to live in dark places where they scavenge the dead bodies of other organisms.

SPANISH FLY
(Lytta vesicatoria)

The so-called Spanish fly is part of a group of beetles called the blister beetles. Their color serves as a warning to predatory birds that they are able to produce toxic chemicals.

The Spanish fly was given its common name by medieval medicine men who stole the poisonous secretions produced by this species to make special potions. In ancient China, this secretion was mixed with human waste to make the world's first ever stink bomb.

LENGTH: Up to .79 in.

FOUND IN: Southern Europe and Central Asia

DIET: Woody plants; larvae feed upon bees

FRENCH GUIANA TUMBLING FLOWER BEETLE
(Variimorda pustulosa)

This beetle is known for its impressive knack for escape. If attacked or cornered by a predatory bird it leaps from its perch and, by flicking its legs as it falls, it spins and tumbles through the air. In all, 1,500 species of tumbling flower beetle have been discovered from habitats around the world. All species depend on this life-saving trick.

The French Guiana tumbling flower beetle is rarely seen and remains mysterious. A future generation of insect scientists is needed to learn more about where it lives and breeds.

LENGTH: Approximately .2–.4 in.

FOUND IN: Rainforests of French Guiana

DIET: Likely to feed on flower pollen

SPOTTED HAIRY FUNGUS BEETLE
(Mycetophagus quadriguttatus)

Both the larvae and the adults of the spotted hairy fungus beetle live in dark, moist areas underneath bark and fallen logs. Here they seek out tender fungus upon which to feed, using scissoring mouthparts common to most beetles.

Although the spotted hairy fungus beetle does an important job of recycling soil nutrients, it is one of many beetles that can occasionally contaminate human food by finding its way into grain stores. For this reason, some scientists like to keep a close eye on where this species occurs.

LENGTH: .12–.16 in.

DIET: Fungus

FOUND IN: Throughout Africa, North America, Australia, Europe, and many parts of Asia

MEALWORM BEETLE
(Tenebrio molitor)

The mealworm beetle is one of the most farmed of all insects. In many parts of the world, their larvae (called mealworms) are eaten as a delicacy. Pound-for-pound, mealworms contain many of the same minerals and vitamins found in meats such as beef, but they are much cheaper to produce.

There may be other uses for mealworms. In 2015, for instance, it was discovered that mealworms are able to digest polystyrene cups, offering a potential solution in the human war against plastic waste.

LENGTH: .47–.71 in.

DIET: Fresh and decaying vegetation

FOUND IN: Originally likely to be a Mediterranean species; now found worldwide

CHECKERED BEETLES (COLEOPTERA)

The checkered beetles are an adaptable group of beetles, made up of approximately 3,500 species. Some species feast on pollen, while other species prefer to seek out dead and dying animals. Many species are predators of other beetles and their larvae. All checkered beetles have long bodies covered with tiny bristling hairs.

RED-LEGGED HAM BEETLE
(Necrobia rufipes)

The red-legged ham beetle spends most of its time looking for decomposing animals. To find a body to scavenge, the red-legged ham beetle locates and homes in on the smell that decay produces. Its larvae bore into the bodies of dead organisms, seeking out maggots to feed upon. Adults hunt maggots nearer the surface.

The red-legged ham beetle is also attracted to other things that give off strong smells. These include cheese, dried eggs, and even dog food. There is even evidence of this species finding its way into the corpses of Egyptian mummies.

LENGTH: .14–.28 in.

DIET: Fly larvae

FOUND IN: Found almost everywhere—one of the world's most cosmopolitan insects

ANT BEETLE
(Thanasimus formicarius)

The ant beetle is a code-cracker. To find its prey of bark beetles, it uses its antennae to sense for the secret scent molecules that bark beetles use to communicate among themselves. By following these scent trails, it follows a path to its dinner. Specialized mouthparts allow the ant beetle to bite through the armored exoskeleton of the bark beetle.

Even ant beetle larvae are specialized hunters of bark beetles. The larvae bore through wood, looking for the tunnels (called "galleries") that bark beetle larvae create.

LENGTH: Up to .4 in.

DIET: Bark beetles and their larvae

FOUND IN: European woodlands where bark beetles are common

YELLOW-HORNED CLERID BEETLE

(Trogodendron fasciculatum)

The yellow-horned clerid beetle runs with urgency up and down logs and branches, flicking its antennae in a manner that makes it look like a wasp. This impressive mimicry keeps spiders from attacking, because the spiders assume it is a predatory wasp that might hunt them. This kind of defensive adaptation (called Batesian mimicry) is common in many insects.

The yellow-horned clerid beetle hunts other insects, including beetles. Its large eyes are used to spot prey from a distance.

LENGTH: .79 in.

FOUND IN: Throughout Australia

DIET: Insects, including larvae of jewel beetles and longhorn beetles

FOUR-SPOTTED CHECKERED BEETLE

(Pelonides quadripunctata)

The four-spotted checkered beetle is a frequent visitor to trees, where it moves among flowers feeding on pollen and the insects that these flowers attract. It may be that its spots confuse potential predators into thinking that it is a poisonous ladybug. This is another example of Batesian mimicry.

Like other checkered beetles, the antennae of the four-spotted checkered beetle are heavily notched, often looking like the antlers of a deer. The notches in the antennae work like a television aerial, helping this beetle pick up as many passing scent molecules as possible.

LENGTH: .16–.31 in.

FOUND IN: Sunny woodlands throughout parts of North America

DIET: Pollen and insects

WEEVIL BEETLES (COLEOPTERA)

Weevils are one of the most successful parts of the beetle family. In total, more than 97,000 species are known. Most species have an impressively long snout with tiny mouthparts on the end—this is called a rostrum. Their habit of eating leaves means that farmers consider some weevil species as pests.

ACORN WEEVIL
(Curculio glandium)

The female acorn weevil uses her incredibly long rostrum to chew tiny grooves into the surface of acorns. Once she has eaten enough, she uses her long abdomen to lay eggs within these grooves. Like all weevils, her abdomen is long and pointed like a wasp's ovipositor. This helps her lay eggs in hard-to-reach places.

As the acorn heals itself, her eggs become sealed-off from predators and parasites. Her babies live as grubs through the winter, insulated from the freezing weather in their cozy acorn home before climbing out as adults the following spring.

LENGTH: .16–.31 in.

FOUND IN: Throughout North America

DIET: Acorns

GIRAFFE WEEVIL
(Trachelophorus giraffa)

This peculiar weevil is named for its extraordinarily protruding head. In males, the long "neck" is used for fighting with other males during the mating season, but this unusual adaptation also comes in handy for both males and females when building their nests. By curling a leaf into a makeshift tent, the female and male giraffe weevils make a protected room in which she lays a single egg that will, in time, feed upon the leaf. The neck can be used like a long finger to fold the leaf over.

LENGTH: Males up to .98 in.; females up to .59 in.

FOUND IN: The rainforests of Madagascar

DIET: The leaves of flowering plants

EUSOCIAL WEEVIL
(Austroplatypus incompertus)

The eusocial weevil is the first beetle known to have gone the way of the ant. Each weevil nest has a single queen responsible for laying eggs, who is tended to by an army of daughters who exist only to serve her.

Scientists also think that this may be the world's oldest animal species capable of farming. These weevils create special tunnels within the bark of eucalyptus within which they grow a special fungus that keeps the colony alive. They are likely to have done this for more than 90 million years.

LENGTH: .24 in.

DIET: Fungus

FOUND IN: The Australian eucalyptus forests of New South Wales and Victoria

RHIGUS WEEVIL
(Rhigus nigrosparsus)

No one appears to know quite why this South American weevil displays such bright colors. It may be that this beetle uses its colors for display or that it tricks birds and spiders into thinking that it is poisonous. Recent teams of scientists investigating South America's precious rainforests hope to find out.

Like all weevils, *Rhigus nigrosparsus* has antennae that are kinked in the middle, making them look like human elbows. Some species can move their antennae into special grooves to keep them out of the way when poking their rostrum into hard-to-reach places.

LENGTH: .87 in.

DIET: Plants

FOUND IN: Rainforests of Brazil and Paraguay

LEAF BEETLES (COLEOPTERA)

The leaf beetle family includes more than 37,000 species. All leaf beetles and their larvae eat plants, particularly leaves. Although this means some species are considered pests by humans, some leaf beetle species can be used to remove or control problem plants that have escaped into the wild.

MOTTLED TORTOISE BEETLE
(Deloyala guttata)

Tortoise beetles get their common name from the tough shell that covers their head and mouthparts. This armor allows them to feed in private, without fear of predators getting to them.

Like many tortoise beetles, the mottled tortoise beetle is able to alter the colors of the metallic patches upon its elytra. Scientists are still working out whether this is an adaptation that makes the beetle look like a leaf covered by dew drops or whether it somehow confuses predators into leaving them alone in some other mysterious way.

LENGTH: Approximately .2 in.

FOUND IN: Throughout the Americas, including the Caribbean

DIET: Leaves

DEAD-NETTLE LEAF BEETLE
(Chrysolina fastuosa)

Many people consider the dead-nettle leaf beetle to be one of the world's most beautiful beetles. Its metallic green elytra mean that sightings are prized by beetle-spotters.

The dead-nettle leaf beetle belongs to a group of leaf beetles often used as a pest-control service, because they eat plants that many humans consider to be weeds. In the last 100 years, leaf beetles like these were introduced to parts of North America and Australia to control plants that had accidentally hitched a lift from Europe and had spread wildly.

LENGTH: .2–.28 in.

FOUND IN: Across Europe

DIET: Dead leaves of nettle plants

FLEA BEETLE
(Psylliodes napi)

When disturbed, this tiny leaf beetle can leap like a flea to safety. Its jumping power comes from an especially large rear pair of legs that resemble those of a grasshopper. Like many leaf beetles, this species of flea beetle is an excellent flyer and frequently moves from plant to plant in search of food.

Some species of flea beetle are unable to fly in rainy weather and seek shelter in the soil on the forest floor. For this reason, German scientists call this group of beetles *Erdflöhe*, which means "earth fleas."

LENGTH: .09–.13 in.

FOUND IN: Throughout Europe, northern Asia, and North America

DIET: Leaves of plants such as cabbage and swede

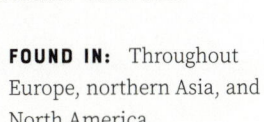

AGGIE BRUCHID
(Megacerus leucospilus)

The aggie bruchid and its close family are often called "seed beetles" because of their habit of spending much of their lives hidden within seeds. Larvae hatch out from eggs laid by adults on the surface of the seed and then munch their way into the center, where they feed in safety without fear of predators.

Seed beetles were once thought to be weevils, but microscopic examination of their bodies has led scientists to consider them to be a strange and important part of the leaf beetle family.

LENGTH: .13–.16 in.

FOUND IN: North and Central America

DIET: Flowering plants

PLEASING FUNGUS BEETLES AND FLAT-BARK BEETLES (COLEOPTERA)

Although numerous, the secretive habits of the pleasing fungus beetles and the flat-bark beetles make them hard to spot and, often, very hard for beetle-spotters to identify. Thousands of species of both types are known. Many species favor woodlands and forests, hiding under logs and fallen branches.

PLEASING FUNGUS BEETLE
(Megalodacne heros)

Adults of this species of pleasing fungus beetle are sometimes seen feeding on fungus alongside their larvae. Together, the adults and their young gnaw on the brackets of fungus that grow on the sides of trees. This is highly unusual behavior for an insect—often the larvae and adults do not eat the same things.

In some years, when dry weather delays the growth of the bracket fungi on which this species depends, many pleasing fungus beetles seek shelter under dead trees. There they wait in large groups for summer rain, which encourages the fungus to grow.

LENGTH: .87 in.

FOUND IN: Woodlands and forests of North America

DIET: Fungus

SLENDER LIZARD BEETLE
(Acropteroxys gracilis)

The female slender lizard beetle uses her keen antennae to seek out a type of flowering plant called ragweed. Upon the plant, a male is waiting. Once her eggs are fertilized, she visits each plant stem, depositing a single egg from which a larva will hatch before tunneling downward to seek food and shelter within the plant.

Because ragweed grows quickly and can compete with crops in farmland, slender lizard beetles are a species that many farmers have come to love. By destroying ragweeds while feeding, these tireless insects offer us a helping hand in our war against weeds.

LENGTH: .24–.47 in.

FOUND IN: Central and North America

DIET: Ragwort plants

FLAT-BARK BEETLE
(Palaestes abruptus)

Because the remote rainforests in which this species lives are so hard to explore, *Palaestes abruptus* is one of many flat-bark beetle species that remain a mystery to scientists. Its larvae have never been seen. Scientists think they are likely to live and feed within the bark of trees.

Adult males of this species are armed with large and very sharp mandibles (mouthparts used for biting and crushing food), which are likely to be used in battles during the breeding season. As with stag beetles, males may wrestle with one another to prove their strength to nearby females seeking a mate.

LENGTH: Up to approximately 1 in.

FOUND IN: Central and South America

DIET: Unknown

RED FLAT-BARK BEETLE
(Cucujus clavipes)

More than perhaps any other insect, the red flat-bark beetle is able to survive even the coldest of winter nights. As the nights grow colder, it starves itself of water so that its body cannot freeze and shatter. Any water that remains in its body is pumped with a special antifreeze chemical that lowers the temperature at which ice crystals can form, limiting the damage that the cold can cause. In this hibernationlike state, the beetle sees out the winter months unharmed until spring returns.

LENGTH: .39–.55 in.

DIET: Sap and insects

FOUND IN: Often found within ash and poplar trees throughout northern parts of the US and Canada

LONGHORN BEETLES (COLEOPTERA)

The longhorn beetles are named after their long antennae which, in some cases, can be longer than the beetle's body. Their larvae (called roundheaded borers) feed and grow within trees. Approximately 26,000 species of longhorn beetles are known from habitats all around the world.

TITAN BEETLE
(Titanus giganteus)

With a body longer than a human hand, the titan beetle is a beast among beetles. Its sharp, hooked mandibles are used in self-defense or to scare off rivals, and it has one of the most powerful bites of any beetle—in a single bite, its jaws are said to be able to snap a pencil in two.

Though this is one of the world's largest beetles, the larva of this species has never been seen. Some scientists think this wood-boring baby life stage may be as long as 12 in.

LENGTH: Adults up to 6.57 in.

DIET: Unknown

FOUND IN: The rainforests of Brazil, Colombia, Ecuador, the Guianas, and Venezuela

GIANT AFRICAN LONGHORN BEETLE
(Petrognatha gigas)

The giant African longhorn beetle searches for fallen branches of acacia trees upon which it lays its eggs. By standing deadly still and using its antennae to mimic the twigs of trees, it manages to blend in totally with its surroundings. This camouflage behavior keeps it safe from predators such as birds and lizards.

Many longhorn beetles rely on camouflage like this to stay hidden. Some species also resemble stinging ants, bees, and wasps.

LENGTH: 7.87 in., including antennae

DIET: Acacia

FOUND IN: Central Africa

ALPINE LONGHORN BEETLE
(Rosalia alpina)

Exuberant patches of blues and blacks adorn the elytra of the alpine longhorn. These patterns match the mottled markings and scratches found upon its host plant, the European beech tree.

In spring, males gather on these trees and sing a simple rasping song by scraping their legs against their wing cases. Incoming females mate with the most impressive males before laying eggs on the bark from which larvae will later hatch. As with many longhorns, the larvae will live within the bark for three years or more before emerging as adults.

LENGTH: .6–1.5 in.

FOUND IN: Throughout Europe

DIET: Adults feed on pollen

HUHU BEETLE
(Prionoplus reticularis)

For many years, the native people of New Zealand have collected and eaten the larvae of the huhu beetle, a white grub that reaches 2.8 in. in length. It is said to taste like chicken mixed with peanut butter.

Although the huhu beetle is New Zealand's heaviest beetle, it has no problems flying. Upon broad wings, it flutters through the night sky, guided by the moon as it searches for a mate.

LENGTH: 1.6–2 in.

FOUND IN: New Zealand

DIET: Larvae feed within conifer trees

MEGALOPTERANS (MEGALOPTERA)

The megalopterans are a prehistoric group of flying insects with broad wings. Today, 300 species are known and all species live in and around wetlands, where eggs and larvae are found. Though larvae may live for many years underwater, adults often live only a matter of days or hours.

EASTERN DOBSONFLY
(Corydalus cornutus)

Like a walrus, the male eastern dobsonfly has long tusklike mandibles. These mandibles are so long they cannot be used in self-defense to bite. Scientists think that, instead, they serve as an advertisement of their strength to females—rather like the tail of a peacock. Males of many dobsonfly species also give a special gift to females—a blob of nutritious slime, which she may consider eating.

The larvae of this species play an important role in freshwater food chains by feeding upon smaller soft-bodied invertebrates. With large eyes and strong mandibles, these hungry larvae grab at young mayflies, stoneflies, and mosquitoes. They spend up to three years in this larval form before pupating at the water's edge. Unusually for insects, the legs and mandibles of the eastern dobsonfly stick out from the pupa as metamorphosis takes place.

WINGSPAN: Up to 5 in.

DIET: Adults do not feed

FOUND IN: Fast-flowing unpolluted streams on North America's eastern side

SUMMER FISHFLY
(Chauliodes pectinicornis)

The summer fishfly lays its eggs on leaves that hang over the water's edge. Once the larvae hatch, they dive into the water to begin their life as an aquatic predator. There they will live for three years or so, feeding upon invertebrates and larger animals, including tadpoles and small fish.

Fishflies resemble dobsonflies, but males do not possess the same giant mandibles. Instead, the male's antennae are noticeably fluffy, a bit like those of some moths. This is to help them detect and track nearby females.

WINGSPAN: 2.36–3.15 in.

DIET: Adults do not feed

FOUND IN: Ponds, marshes, and swamps across North America's eastern side

MUD ALDERFLY
(Sialis lutaria)

Sialis lutaria is an alderfly species common through the wetlands of Europe. Its larvae are skilled predators armed with powerful jaws. They breathe underwater using rows of feathery gills on their abdomen.

Though closely related to fishflies and dobsonflies, alderflies do not have extra eyes on the roof of their head. Alderflies are also poor fliers. This means that, unlike most megalopterans, many adult alderflies have to stay around the same body of water from which they hatched as larvae.

WINGSPAN: .87–1.42 in.

FOUND IN: Europe

DIET: Adults do not feed

CADDISFLIES (TRICHOPTERA)

Caddisflies are small mothlike insects with wings that are covered in tiny hairs. They are best known for their spectacular larvae, many of which create special cases out of underwater detritus to keep themselves safe. Scientists have discovered more than 14,500 species in total.

NORTHERN CASEMAKER CADDISFLY
(Nemotaulius hostilis)

Like most caddisflies, the larva of the northern casemaker caddisfly weaves silk to make a sticky cloak upon which a leaf can be glued. This gives the larva protection as it grows. The northern casemaker caddisfly larva is described as a "leaf-shredder"—its mouthparts slice up old leaves before digestion begins.

After pupating, adult males of this caddisfly species use their long antennae to detect other caddisflies so that egg-laying can take place. Within hours of mating, many adults die of exhaustion.

LENGTH: .87 in.

DIET: Larvae feed upon leaves

FOUND IN: Rivers, lakes, and small streams in North America

BLACK DANCER
(Mystacides sepulchralis)

In the summer months, great swarms of black dancers congregate at the water's edge. Within these busy clouds, males and females approach one another to mate before dropping down to the water surface to lay eggs. Not every male will be successful. Many adults fall into the water and drown and some become entangled in spiders' webs.

Their larvae make a protective case from stones and seeds found on the water bottom. This camouflaged costume makes the larva of the black dancer very hard for passing fish and invertebrate predators to spot.

LENGTH: .31 in. body length

FOUND IN: Throughout North America

DIET: Rotting pond plants

LEPTOCERUS INTERRUPTUS

This species is so rare that it has not yet been given a common name by scientists. It is one of a group of caddisflies called "long-horned caddisflies" because of the hairlike antennae that are often longer than the insect's body.

The larvae of *Leptocerus interruptus* live among the tree roots at the edges of large slow-flowing rivers. This species requires clean, unpolluted water to survive and grow. Because of human activities, habitats like these are harder and harder to find. This may explain why the species has become so rare.

LENGTH: Approximately .2–.4 in.

FOUND IN: Isolated clean rivers across Europe

DIET: Unknown

LAND CADDIS
(Enoicyla pusilla)

The land caddis is the only caddisfly species to explore a world away from the water. Its larvae live among fallen leaves on the forest floor. To protect themselves from the dry air, these larvae weave a protective blanket out of silk which they cover with fine sand.

Unlike other caddisflies, the female land caddis does not have true wings. She remains unable to fly for her entire life. The male will use his long antennae to locate her among patches of undergrowth beneath old oak trees.

LENGTH: .79 in.

FOUND IN: Oak woodlands across Europe

DIET: Larvae feed on old oak leaves

DAY-FLYING MOTHS (LEPIDOPTERA)

Planet Earth is home to almost 180,000 species of moth. Like butterflies, moths are mostly nectar-feeding insects with wings and bodies covered with tiny scales, which look like dust to our human eyes. Although most moths are nocturnal, flying at night, some moths fly in the daylight hours.

HANDMAIDEN MOTH
(Amata bicincta)

The handmaiden moth is a part of a large family of moths able to produce sounds using their abdomen. These sounds can be used to block out the clicking noises that bats use to hunt, making the moth harder to detect. Moths of this family can also use their abdomen to sing simple love songs to one another.

Like many day-flying moths, the handmaiden moth uses bright colors to warn predators of its disgusting taste. The hairy caterpillar larvae of this moth and its close relatives are often known as "woolly bears."

WINGSPAN: 1.06 in.

DIET: Nectar

FOUND IN: Known from the Himalayas and other nearby regions

FIRE GRID BURNET
(Arniocera erythropyga)

Birds and lizards learn not to mess with the fire grid burnet. This day-flying moth is able to turn the chemicals in its food into hydrogen cyanide, one of the most poisonous molecules known. Even its caterpillar stages are highly poisonous and are avoided by predators.

As with most moths, the fire grid burnet holds its colorful wings against its body when resting. Its long featherlike antennae are used by males and females to locate one another during the breeding season.

WINGSPAN: .98–1.2 in.

DIET: Nectar

FOUND IN: Southern Africa

HUMMINGBIRD HAWKMOTH

(Macroglossum stellatarum)

The hummingbird hawkmoth can beat its wings an incredible 85 times each second. It dips its long tongue (or proboscis) into trumpetlike flowers and sucks out the sugary nectar it requires to power this high-energy lifestyle. The hummingbird hawkmoth's ability to hover and dart busily from flower to flower and the long featherlike hairs on its abdomen mean that people regularly confuse this insect with a real hummingbird.

Unlike most moths, the hummingbird hawkmoth uses its eyes to locate the freshest flowers. These eyes are very sensitive to bright colors, and during its lifetime each individual hummingbird hawkmoth is able to learn which color of flower produces the richest nectar.

This species is among the most well traveled of moths. Each year, individuals regularly move across Europe and Asia, crossing oceans and seas in their search for nectar.

WINGSPAN: 1.6–1.77 in.

DIET: Nectar

FOUND IN: Throughout Europe and Asia during summer months

MICROMOTHS (LEPIDOPTERA)

Of the 180,000 moth species known to scientists, approximately 50,000 are called "micromoths." Micromoths have a wingspan of less than 1 in. and are often very difficult to tell apart. Although they are easy to overlook, micromoths play an important role on planet Earth. Many species pollinate flowers that other insects cannot.

BIRD CHERRY ERMINE
(Yponomeuta evonymella)

Because it is so small, people rarely see the adult bird cherry ermine moth in flight, yet its caterpillars are unmistakable. By leaving a trail of silk wherever this caterpillar moves, each individual caterpillar begins to create a spiderlike webbing over the leaves and branches near its home. Over time, this provides the caterpillars with an insect "force field" that gives them safety from predators. Beneath their protective silk blanket, the caterpillars strip the tree entirely of its leaves before pupating.

WINGSPAN: .6–1 in.

FOUND IN: Across Europe and Asia

DIET: Caterpillars feed upon bird cherry trees

COMMON CLOTHES MOTH
(Tineola bisselliella)

The secret of the common clothes moth's success comes from its adaptable nature. Long before humans, the caterpillars of the common clothes moth fed upon the fur of animals, both alive and dead. In the modern day, however, this species has changed its diet. Today, it feeds upon fabrics that are used in human clothes, particularly those that contain wool. Occasionally this species also feeds on grains and other human food. This makes it a species some would consider a pest.

WINGSPAN: .35–.63 in.

DIET: Clothes, grains, fur

FOUND IN: Originally found in Europe and Asia; now found worldwide

MORNING-GLORY PLUME MOTH

(Emmelina monodactyla)

Unlike most micromoths, the morning-glory plume moth rolls up the front edges of its wings when it lands and holds them aloft like a glider. When it has rested enough, it flies through gardens and woodlands seeking out flowers with lots of nectar.

Though small in size, the morning-glory plume moth is one of the toughest of all micromoths. Individuals regularly see out the winter months without succumbing to icy winds, rain, and snow. This means that, unusually for moths, adults of this species can be seen throughout the year.

WINGSPAN: .7–1.1 in.

FOUND IN: Throughout most of the Northern Hemisphere

DIET: Nectar

HAWAIIAN LEAF-MINER

(Philodoria succedanea)

The islands of Hawai'i are a bountiful place for secretive micromoths like the Hawaiian leaf-miner. Many of the species that live there are very closely related and each species depends upon a different native plant species for its caterpillars to feed upon.

Because the Hawaiian islands are changing so quickly due to climate change and the introduction of exotic plants and animals, the native plants that micromoths like this depend upon are disappearing. This means that many of Hawai'i's micromoths are sliding toward extinction.

WINGSPAN: .31 in.

FOUND IN: The Hawaiian islands of Kauai, Oahu, Lanai, Maui, and Hawai'i

DIET: Caterpillars live within the leaves of hibiscus plants

MEGA MOTHS (LEPIDOPTERA)

Some moth species have wingspans that rival birds. The large size of these moths requires powerful flight muscles. This gives their bodies a far rounder shape. Because of the unmistakable beauty of these insects, the largest moths are often admired and celebrated by insect-lovers the world over.

ATLAS MOTH
(Attacus atlas)

With a wingspan of up to a foot in length, the Atlas moth is one of the world's largest insects. It could sit quite comfortably on a human arm and it is too big for many birds to try and catch.

Large size brings problems for flying insects, because it means they require lots of energy to get off the ground. For this reason, the Atlas moth spends much of its time resting in the treetops while looking out for mates. As with many moths, the female is able to release special chemicals into the air (called pheromones), which males detect using their sensitive antennae. Males follow these scent trails to the waiting female so that egg-laying can begin.

WINGSPAN: 9.8–12 in.

FOUND IN: Forests of Asia

DIET: Adults do not feed; caterpillars feed on citrus, cinnamon, and guava trees, as well as evergreen trees

DOMESTIC SILKMOTH
(Bombyx mori)

Just as goats, sheep and horses have been domesticated by humans to perform important jobs, so too have some insects. The domestic silkmoth was taken from the wild 5,000 years ago in China and bred by humans, who collected the silk produced by its caterpillar, called the silkworm.

Today, domestic silkmoth caterpillars are fed mulberry leaves to help them produce the silk used in modern clothes and fabrics. It takes 194 lbs of mulberry leaves and 2,500 silkworms to produce a single pound of silk.

WINGSPAN: 1.2–2 in.

DIET: Mulberry leaves

FOUND IN: Reared in captivity throughout the world

HORNET MOTH
(Sesia apiformis)

The hornet moth's clear wings and stripy body give it the appearance of a large hornet. This is a spectacular example of so-called Batesian mimicry, when insects look like deadly animals so that they can scare away predators. The moth is even said to fly like a wasp in a zig-zagging pattern, further convincing predatory birds to steer clear.

As with other large moth species, the hornet moth's adult life stage is only a matter of days.

WINGSPAN: 1.34–2 in.

DIET: Their wood-boring caterpillars are often found on aspen, willow and poplar trees

FOUND IN: Throughout Europe and the Middle East

BEAUTIFUL BUTTERFLIES
(LEPIDOPTERA)

Butterflies are among the most colorful of insects. Many species use bright blues, reds, and greens to tell one another apart. Their bright colors are made by lots of microscopic scales on their wings. These scales reflect light from the sun like thousands of tiny mirrors.

MENELAUS BLUE MORPHO
(Morpho menelaus)

There are few colors in nature quite like the blue wings of the Menelaus blue morpho. The banding patterns on each of the microscopic scales that adorn its wings scatter light in different directions, meaning that its wings appear to change color as they move. This is called iridescence.

So colorful and unique is this butterfly, that for more than a century it was hunted by amateur naturalists eager to acquire the most colorful specimens for their collections. This, along with deforestation, has led to their numbers plummeting in some parts of South America.

WINGSPAN: 4.72 in.

FOUND IN: Central and South America

DIET: Rotting fruit

AMBER PHANTOM
(Haetera piera)

The clear wings of the amber phantom work like a cloak of invisibility that keeps it hidden from predators. This species spends most of its time hiding among leaves on the floor of the forest, choosing to fly only at dusk and dawn.

The amber phantom and its close relatives are known for their unusual habit of perching on four legs, rather than six. Some scientists think this frees up two of their legs so they can be used to waft pheromones further into the air to advertise their whereabouts to nearby males or females.

WINGSPAN: 1.6–2 in.

FOUND IN: Throughout many tropical regions of South America

DIET: Rotting fruits on the forest floor

QUEEN ALEXANDRA'S BIRDWING

(Ornithoptera alexandrae)

With a wingspan almost as wide as the open pages of this book, the Queen Alexandra's birdwing is the largest butterfly on our planet. Its large size and powerful wing muscles make it hard for most other animals to catch and eat it. Only the largest spiders and birds stand a chance.

As with many butterflies, adult males and females of this species do not look the same. The males have iridescent markings upon their wings and females have brown wings with white markings.

When a male Queen Alexandra's birdwing spots a female, it flutters over and hovers above her while releasing a special "love potion" of chemicals that helps her begin producing eggs.

The Queen Alexandra's birdwing is so spectacularly beautiful that the species has become highly sought after by collectors. To protect this wonderful insect from extinction, scientists have made it illegal to capture or sell this species. It is one of only four insects in the world to have been protected in this way. The other three protected species are swallowtail butterflies, traditionally captured and traded for their long wings and eye-catching colors.

WINGSPAN: 9.8 in.

FOUND IN: Forests of eastern Papua New Guinea

DIET: Nectar

MASTERS OF CAMOUFLAGE (LEPIDOPTERA)

Moths and butterflies have many predators, including birds, bats, and lizards. For this reason, many species have evolved impressive camouflage patterns to help them blend in with their surroundings.

ORANGE OAKLEAF
(Kallima inachus)

On the side of a tree in the middle of the day, a brown leaf stirs and flutters in an unusual way. The apparent leaf opens up wide into a set of bright orange wings and a butterfly flies off and disappears into the sky. This is the disguise of the orange oakleaf, a species with wings that mimic the color, texture, and veins on decaying leaves. The disguise is so good that even the scientists who study this species are regularly fooled.

WINGSPAN: 3.35–4.33 in.

FOUND IN: Tropical parts of Asia

DIET: Fruits and tree sap

COMMA BUTTERFLY
(Polygonia c-album)

The comma butterfly uses two forms of camouflage in its lifetime. As an adult, its wings look like nibbled or decaying leaves, helping it to blend in among the leaf litter of the forest floor. As a caterpillar, it uses a different form of camouflage. After hatching from its egg, it develops a long black and white marking along the topmost side of its body. This helps it look to passing predators like a disgusting bird dropping. Naturally, birds steer clear of the caterpillars of the comma butterfly.

WINGSPAN: Approximately 1.8 in.

FOUND IN: Europe, Asia, and North Africa

DIET: Nectar

BUFF-TIP
(Phalera bucephala)

This unusual moth gets its name from the fact that it looks like the tip of a developing twig on the side of a branch. The rounded shape of its head even resembles the sphere-shaped bud of a twig in springtime.

During the day, the buff-tip stays deadly still to remain unnoticed by predators. Only once the sun sets will it take to the sky to look for the special trees upon which it lays its eggs.

WINGSPAN: 2.16–2.68 in.

FOUND IN: Throughout Europe and Asia

DIET: Larvae feed on trees including maple, oak, willow, hazel, and birch

PEPPERED MOTH
(Biston betularia)

The peppered moth is a master of adaptation. During the Industrial Revolution, when air pollution made tree trunks black with soot, the peppered moth evolved. Darker forms of this species blended in with the soot-colored trees extremely well and were harder for predatory birds to spot. The lighter-colored moths, however, were easily preyed upon. Over time, the peppered moth's color shifted from white to black.

This is one of the most famous examples of evolution in action, a demonstration of Charles Darwin's big idea known as natural selection.

WINGSPAN: 1.38–2.36 in.

FOUND IN: Throughout shrublands and forests across much of Europe, Asia, and North America

DIET: Nectar and rotting fruits

AUDACIOUS EYESPOTS
(LEPIDOPTERA)

While many butterflies and moths depend on camouflage to stay safe, many other species have evolved complicated eyespots that are celebrated and admired by human cultures all over the world. Scientists are still investigating what these eyespots do. In some cases, the eyespots may scare a predator into thinking a bigger animal is looking back at them.

IO MOTH
(Automeris io)

When resting on the side of a tree, the io moth hides its eyespots with its first pair of wings. Should a predator approach, the io moth opens up its wings quickly to reveal a pair of dazzlingly large eyespots that shock the predator and scare it away.

Like its close relatives, the adults of this moth species hatch from their pupae without mouthparts and do not feed as adults. All of the energy the io moth burns up in its adult life, it collects during the caterpillar life stage.

WINGSPAN: 2.5–3.5 in.

FOUND IN: Throughout North America

DIET: Leaves of many plant species

EUROPEAN PEACOCK
(Aglais io)

Unlike many butterflies, the European peacock hibernates during the winter months. During this time, it folds its wings together and stays deadly still to mimic a dried-up leaf. Should a hungry bird approach during the winter, the butterfly opens its wings to reveal four dramatic eyespots.

Scientists have tested how good these eyespots are for scaring predators away and concluded that the defence works best against small birds.

The European peacock has another defense for hungry rats and mice—it produces an intimidating hiss like a snake.

WINGSPAN: 2–2.2 in.

FOUND IN: Throughout Europe and Asia

DIET: Nectar

COMET MOTH
(Argema mittrei)

The comet moth's unusual eyespot patterns are mostly used to scare off birds and lizards that disturb it during the day while it rests. At night, when the comet moth flies, it faces a different predator—bats.

Eyespots do not work against bats because these predators hunt at night when there is less light. To stop this predator from attacking, the comet moth has evolved a different adaptation. The long trailing plumes on the tips of the comet moth's wings spin as they fly, confusing the bat into attacking the moth's tail rather than its head.

WINGSPAN: Approximately 7.9 in.

FOUND IN: Rainforests of Madagascar

DIET: Caterpillars feed on a range of Madagascan trees

FOREST GIANT OWL
(Caligo eurilochus)

The forest giant owl hides among leaves during the day and takes to the sky upon large fluttering wings only at dusk and dawn. Its eyespots are thought to mimic the other predators active at this time, especially owls.

Because of its beautiful eyespots, the forest giant owl is one of the world's most celebrated butterflies. So proud is Brazil of this unusual species, it once used an image of it on the nation's stamps.

WINGSPAN: 8 in.

FOUND IN: Throughout tropical regions of Central and South America

DIET: Fruits and animal manure

MAMMOTH MIGRATORS (LEPIDOPTERA)

Butterflies and moths are among the most well traveled of insects. By moving on the winds, many species can migrate hundreds or thousands of miles in search of food plants upon which to lay eggs. Scientists are very interested in how butterflies and moths manage this.

MONARCH BUTTERFLY
(Danaus plexippus)

The monarch butterfly is one of the world's most celebrated migrant insects. Each spring, in great swarms, hundreds of thousands of them make their way north from Mexico toward the US and Canada.

As it moves, the monarch butterfly regularly drops down to the forest floor to lay eggs on plants. These eggs hatch into caterpillars and, later, a new generation of monarch butterflies will continue the journey northward. In this way, the movement of this butterfly species across North America resembles athletes running a relay race. When summer ends, the monarch butterfly makes its journey back toward the equator, where the species spends the winter months in great sleeping swarms.

Quite how the monarch butterfly manages this epic migration remains a mystery. Scientists suspect that the species may navigate by following trails of special chemicals left by previous generations or that the species has an in-built "sun-clock" that helps it track the changing of the seasons.

WINGSPAN: 3.5–4 in.

DIET: Adults drink nectar; caterpillars feed on milkweed

FOUND IN: From southern Canada to northern South America, as well as isolated islands across the Pacific and Atlantic oceans

DARK BLUE TIGER
(Tirumala septentrionis)

As the monsoon season hits India, the dark blue tiger readies itself for migration. The sudden change of weather and the lack of food cause its body to stop producing eggs. Instead, it stores as much energy as it can for the journey to come.

In vast swarms millions-strong, the dark blue tiger migrates from India's Western Ghats to the Eastern Ghats covering a journey of 250 miles. Here, where plants are less affected by the monsoons, it refills its energy supplies and prepares itself to lay eggs.

WINGSPAN: 3.15–4.5 in.

FOUND IN: Throughout many parts of Asia

DIET: Nectar

PAINTED LADY
(Vanessa cardui)

Thousands of scientists working together have recently discovered the mysterious migrations of the painted lady, one of the most wide-ranging insects on Earth. For many painted lady butterflies, the journey begins in Africa in spring. From here, they swarm northward over Europe and Asia in summer before later generations circle southward back into Africa to see out the winter.

Overall, this epic migration covers 7,500 miles and involves crossing the Sahara Desert not once but twice. This incredible journey makes the painted lady one of the world's toughest travelers.

WINGSPAN: 2–2.2 in.

DIET: Nectar

FOUND IN: Known from every continent except South America and Antarctica

PRIZED POLLINATORS (LEPIDOPTERA)

Many butterflies and moths drink nectar using a long proboscis that resembles a tongue. While drinking nectar, they pick up pollen from the flowers of many plants, which they then carry to other flowers, helping the plants to pollinate. Without butterflies and moths, many plant species would suffer.

MORGAN'S SPHINX MOTH
(Xanthopan morganii)

The Morgan's sphinx moth has one of the longest tongues in nature. It spends much of its time searching for a rare species of orchid that has especially long bucket-shaped flowers. When the moth finds this single species of unusual orchid, it hovers nearby and unrolls a spectacular foot-long proboscis which it carefully dips into the flower to drink.

The orchid is completely dependent on the Morgan's sphinx moth for survival and the moth is dependent on the orchid for nectar. This sort of relationship between organisms is called mutualism.

WINGSPAN: 5.5–6.3 in.

FOUND IN: Remote rainforests of Madagascar

DIET: Nectar from Darwin's orchid

YUCCA MOTH
(Tegeticula yuccasella)

The tiny yucca moth has created a curious friendship with a peculiar group of plants called yuccas. Each of the yucca's small white flowers can only be reached by the yucca moth, which gathers energy from its nectar. To stop the yucca moth going to a different type of flower for its nectar, the yucca produces extra seeds which provide a home for its caterpillars. In return, the yucca gets a free pollination service from the moths.

WINGSPAN: .7–1.1 in.

FOUND IN: Desert regions of North America

DIET: Nectar

GARDENIA BEE HAWK
(Cephonodes kingii)

The Gardenia bee hawk is one of the most energetic of day-flying moths. It zooms from flower to flower, hovering motionless while it unfurls its enormous proboscis to begin feeding. Its long tongue and powerful flight mean it can visit a number of flower species to keep its energy reserves topped up throughout the day.

So large and breathtaking is this species that it is one of a number of moths that are regularly mistaken for large bees or even hummingbirds.

WINGSPAN: 1.57 in.   **FOUND IN:** Northern Australia

DIET: Nectar

LARGE YELLOW UNDERWING
(Noctua pronuba)

Under the cover of darkness and while humans sleep, the large yellow underwing makes its move. In silence it flies through gardens, forests, and farmlands collecting nectar and moving pollen from plant to plant.

In 2018, scientists investigated how much pollen moths like the large yellow underwing carry. In all, the moths were discovered to have carried pollen from 30 different plant species. Research like this suggests that common moths like this one may be as important as bees in helping to pollinate flowers and keep ecosystems healthy.

WINGSPAN: 2–2.36 in.   **FOUND IN:** Throughout Europe, Asia, and North Africa

DIET: Nectar

CHARISMATIC CATERPILLARS
(LEPIDOPTERA)

In many species, butterflies and moths spend months or even years in the caterpillar life stage. This means caterpillars require lots of adaptations to find food and to help stay safe from predators. On these pages we explore some of most world's most charismatic caterpillars.

PUSS MOTH CATERPILLAR
(Cerura vinula)

When spooked by a potential predator, the puss moth caterpillar rears back its head to reveal a pattern that resembles a snake's mouth. If this fails to scare off birds or lizards, the puss moth resorts to a monstrous back-up plan. From out of the tip of its bottom it produces two poison-hoses which spray acid at the eyes of intruders. In many cases, this is likely to be more than enough to scare away even the bravest of its predators.

LENGTH: 2.36 in.

DIET: Willow and poplar plants

FOUND IN: Throughout dense woodlands of Europe, Asia and parts of North Africa

SOUTHERN FLANNEL MOTH CATERPILLAR
(Megalopyge opercularis)

The caterpillars of the southern flannel moth look furry, almost like a miniature mammal. However, rather than providing warmth, its coat of hair is used for protection. Each "hair" is actually a venomous spine, which is connected to a sack of poison in the caterpillar's body. If stroked, poison moves up the spine and is squirted into the body of its attacker.

Many caterpillars depend upon venomous hairs like these to protect themselves. Some species, such as burnet moths, produce a form of highly toxic cyanide.

LENGTH: 1 in.

DIET: Oak, elms, and wild plums

FOUND IN: Across Central America and in many eastern regions of the US

GUM-LEAF SKELETONIZER CATERPILLAR
(Uraba lugens)

Few caterpillars are as ghoulish as that of the gum-leaf skeletonizer. While other caterpillars completely shed their skins as they grow, the gum-leaf skeletonizer holds onto the shed skin around its head and wears it like a little hat, leading to its other nickname, the "mad hatterpillar." Each time it sheds, the caterpillar keeps the previous "heads" so that, in the late stages of its growth, it wears a tower of discarded scalps on the top of its body. Quite what purpose this behavior plays is not yet known. It may be that this strange adaptation scares away predators such as birds.

LENGTH: Approximately .79 in.

FOUND IN: Throughout Australia and New Zealand

DIET: Leaves of eucalyptus trees

HAWAIIAN CARNIVOROUS CATERPILLAR
(Eupithecia monticolens)

The islands of Hawai'i are the only place on Earth where a group of caterpillars have adopted a new way of life and become carnivores. These caterpillars are called 'loopers'—they grab hold of a branch or twig with the rear-end of their body and wait with the front end of their body ready to strike at passing flies. Many years ago, the sharp mouthparts of these caterpillars were used to chew through leaves. Today, they are adapted to bite through their prey's hard exoskeleton.

LENGTH: .2–.8 in.

FOUND IN: Remote forests of Hawai'i

DIET: Flies and other small insects

ROBBER FLIES AND BEE FLIES (DIPTERA)

Earth is home to 125,000 species of fly, although many hundreds of new types are discovered each year. In total, there may be more than a million species that scientists have not yet named. On these pages, we explore flies that are able to fly with precision skill.

YELLOW FEATHERY ANTENNAE ROBBER FLY
(Ommatius coeraebus)

Like an eagle sitting on its perch, the yellow feathery antennae robber fly watches the sky looking for the telltale shapes of passing insects. Its spherical compound eyes allow it to see in many directions at once.

When the yellow feathery antennae robber fly spots unsuspecting prey, it dashes upward and grasps its meal with grappling legs. Like all robber flies, this species has a long daggerlike proboscis used to suck its prey dry. A furry mustache (called the mystax) helps keep its mouthparts protected should its prey attempt to fight back.

LENGTH: .79 in.

FOUND IN: Throughout eastern regions of Australia

DIET: Insects

HYPERALONIA MORIO

Hovering above the entrance to a nest of ants, *Hyperalonia morio* readies herself to drop her payload of eggs. Like tiny bombs, she drops them into the ant nest where they hatch into tiny maggots that feast upon ant larvae.

Hyperalonia morio is one of 4,500 fly species known as bee flies because of their hairy abdomens. Unlike other flying insects, bee flies hold their proboscis out straight in front of them like a long beak while they fly.

LENGTH: Up to 1.6 in.

DIET: Nectar

FOUND IN: Throughout Argentina, Bolivia, Brazil, Chile, Paraguay, and Uruguay

HANGING THIEF
(Diogmites properans)

The hanging thief is one of the most predatory of all flies. It can even capture and overpower large venomous wasps. Like all robber flies, the hanging thief injects special saliva into its prey that paralyzes and kills it. This saliva also contains a chemical that turns insects to mush, meaning the insides can be drunk by the robber fly like a nutritious soup.

The hanging thief eats its meal in athletic style. Once it has captured its meal of flying insects, it returns to a nearby leaf or twig, which it grasps with one or two legs adorned with special grappling hooks. Here, attached to the leaf or twig, it dangles like a monkey while it uses the rest of its leg to stop its prey from wriggling and escaping.

Very little is known of the maggot life stage of this species and the other 7,000 or so described robber fly species. This is partly because their secretive larvae are very good at hiding among leaf litter.

LENGTH: .8–1 in.

DIET: Flying insects

FOUND IN: Woodlands throughout warmer regions of South America and parts of the southern US

HOVERFLIES (DIPTERA)

Flies are insects known for flying upon a single pair, rather than two pairs, of wings. Their speed and agility has made them masters of a number of habitats. Among the fastest and most agile are the family known as hoverflies.

DIMORPHIC BEAR HOVERFLY

(Criorhina berberina)

The dimorphic bear hoverfly gets its name from its tufty hair. This helps it look like a stinging bumblebee and protects it from predatory birds. This fly flits and darts between flowers, hovering carefully to assess how sugar-rich each flower might be. Like other hoverflies, its wings beat with incredible speed while hovering. Scientists think this species can flap its wings 120 times in a single second.

Scientists use the presence of this hoverfly species in woodlands to judge the health of the local ecosystem. The more hoverflies there are, the more healthy the woodland.

LENGTH: .31–.51 in.

DIET: Nectar

FOUND IN: Woodlands throughout Europe and western parts of Asia

BACCHA ELONGATA

A long club-shaped abdomen gives *Baccha elongata* the appearance of a wasp. It can even wiggle its abdomen around as if it has a venomous stinger. The added stripes across the abdomen make the disguise extra foolproof.

Although this hoverfly is common in gardens throughout Europe and North America, *Baccha elongata* is rarely noticed or studied by insect lovers. This is why the species has no common name, only the formal scientific name given to it by the scientists that first described it.

LENGTH: .28–.43 in.

DIET: Nectar

FOUND IN: Throughout North America and Europe

DRONEFLY
(Eristalis tenax)

The dronefly is a world-conquering hoverfly. It thrives in gardens, parks, and fields across nearly every continent on Earth.

The secret of its success is its incredible maggots, which are capable of living underwater in murky puddles and stinky pools. A long tube protruding from the bottom of these maggots acts like a snorkel, meaning they can breathe and feed at the same time. Scientists suspect that these maggots are able to eat the bacteria that thrive there.

LENGTH: .5–.6 in.

FOUND IN: All continents except Antarctica

DIET: Nectar

AMERICAN HOVERFLY
(Eupeodes americanus)

The American hoverfly is an unrecognized superhero among insects. While moving from flower to flower searching for nectar, this species also moves pollen from plant to plant. This helps keep crops healthy and free from disease.

Even its larvae help farmers. These predatory maggots crawl across the underside of leaves seeking out aphids. When an aphid is discovered, the maggot plucks the aphid off the leaf with its piercing mouthparts and then drains its prey of its bodily fluids. Each day, in their millions, these maggots perform a vital pest-control service in North America.

LENGTH: .35–.47 in.

FOUND IN: Flower-filled meadows and fields of North America

DIET: Nectar from flowers

MOSQUITOES, MIDGES AND CRANEFLIES (DIPTERA)

The families of fly that include midges, mosquitoes, and craneflies are one of the richest and most diverse parts of the group of insects known as flies. These groups represent thousands of fly species and exist on all continents on Earth, including Antarctica—they are the only land animals to have colonized this continent.

FROG-BITING MIDGE
(Corethrella brakeleyi)

This species of frog-biting midge listens for a distinctive call coming from the source of its meal, a frog. When it hears the familiar croak, it moves toward the sound, using a special sense organ on the second segment of its antennae to home in as quickly as possible.

When it finds a frog, the frog-biting midge settles down on its skin and begins to suck its blood. Fewer than 100 species of frog-biting midge are known, though the group lives among many types of frog all over the world.

LENGTH: .04–.2 in.

DIET: Frog blood

FOUND IN: Throughout southern states of the US

PHANTOM MIDGE
(Chaoborus punctipennis)

The phantom midge gets its name from its predatory larva, which is completely see-through like a ghost. This larva ambushes tiny crustaceans that live in water. The only thing that gives away its presence is a pair of tiny eyes, a brain, and two pairs of airbags to help it float.

To catch its prey, the phantom midge larva flicks out a basket of bristles from its mouthparts, trapping its meal in a cage from which it cannot escape. The whole action takes just 14 milliseconds, making these the fastest mouthparts of all insects.

LENGTH: Adults .08–.4 in.

DIET: Larvae eat crustaceans; adults do not feed

FOUND IN: Near lakes and ponds throughout North America

PADDLE-LEGGED BEAUTY
(Sabethes cyaneus)

The paddle-legged beauty is the most colorful and showy of known mosquitoes. Its shiny blue sheen and large paddle-like legs are used to show off its health and vigor, making this species one of the few mosquitoes known to display like a peacock.

Like many mosquito species, the paddle-legged beauty is capable of spreading diseases to humans when they feed upon blood. These diseases include yellow fever virus, which kills tens of thousands of people each year.

LENGTH: Adults approximately .8 in.

FOUND IN: Tropical regions of South America

DIET: Blood

MARSH CRANEFLY
(Tipula oleracea)

The marsh cranefly is best known for its maggot, a thumb-sized larva called a leatherjacket, which lives in soil. Leatherjackets regularly munch through the roots of crops, meaning that many farmers consider them a pest. Because a female marsh cranefly can lay up to 1,200 eggs, sometimes whole fields can be destroyed by this species.

Though not closely related to mosquitoes and midges, the craneflies are a fly family that has also trailblazed the world. In all, scientists know of 15,000 species.

LENGTH: Adults 1.4–2.2 in.

FOUND IN: Throughout fields, forests, and gardens across Europe

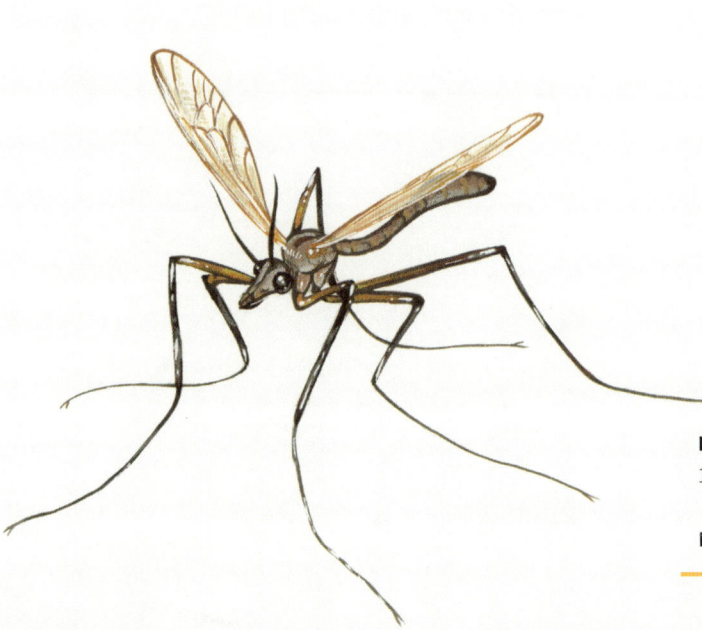

DIET: Nectar

SOLDIER FLIES, AWL-FLIES, AND HORSEFLIES (DIPTERA)

One of the reasons for the success of flies on planet Earth is their diverse tastes and adaptable nature. Though closely related to one another, the fly species on these pages each perform a unique role in their local environment, as do their larvae.

BLACK SOLDIER FLY
(Hermetia illucens)

To avoid being eaten, the black soldier fly wears a disguise. Its antennae are long, like those of a wasp, and two transparent "windows" in its wings give the illusion of it having a thin wasplike waist.

In recent centuries, the black soldier fly has spread across the globe. This is a good thing for soils because the larvae of this species churn their way through leaf litter, digesting nutrients that are then returned to the soil to make it healthy. The species can even be used to compost kitchen scraps.

LENGTH: .63 in.

DIET: Nectar

FOUND IN: Numerous habitats across nearly all continents worldwide

COENOMYIA FERRUGINEA

Coenomyia ferruginea is an awl-fly, one of a small group of fly species that scientists are eager to learn more about. It lives near water, often preferring high altitudes such as hills and mountains. Females are easy to spot because of their large egg-filled abdomens. Once hatched, the larvae of this species move through soil and leaf litter, hunting other insects.

Awl-flies are sometimes known as "stink flies" because they can release an odor when being attacked by predators. The scent these flies produce is said to smell like cheese.

LENGTH: .5–.8 in.

DIET: Nectar and honeydew

FOUND IN: Western Europe, Siberia, and North America

COMMON HORSEFLY
(Haematopota pluvialis)

Many millions of years ago, the horseflies came from a family of nectar-feeders. As time went on, however, this species gained a taste for blood—especially the blood of mammals. To collect its blood meal, the horsefly slashes at the skin with sharp mouthparts before licking the blood that flows out and flying away.

Only the female common horsefly drinks blood in this way, however. She uses this nutritious fluid to power the growth of her eggs. Males obtain energy by drinking nectar from flowers, just as their ancestors once did.

LENGTH: .2–.5 in.

DIET: Males drink nectar; females drink mammal blood

FOUND IN: Damp heaths and moorlands throughout Europe and parts of Asia

HIPPO FLY
(Tabanus biguttatus)

With its enormous wraparound eyes, this horsefly species targets the largest of mammals, particularly cows and hippos. An armored body means that, if squashed or lashed with a tail, the hippo fly can hold onto the skin unharmed. It is said that bites from this fly are one of the reasons that hippos spend so much time underwater.

As with other horseflies, the larvae of this species are adaptable hunters. They move through muddy ponds and pools, feeding on insects and even frog tadpoles, before pupating at the water's edge.

LENGTH: Approximately 2 in.

DIET: Females drink mammal blood

FOUND IN: Southern Africa

DANCE FLIES, LONG-LEGGED FLIES, AND SNAIL-KILLING FLIES (DIPTERA)

The dance flies, the long-legged flies, and the snail-killing flies are three fly groups that scientists are eager to learn more about. Each group has its own fascinating behaviors that are unlike any other insect in this book. These behaviors include dancing, flag-waving, and snail-hunting.

OCYDROMIA GLABRICULA

In dense clouds of activity, hundreds of thousands of *Ocydromia glabricula* get together to mate. To entice and attract a female, males of this species dance in a special way while flying. For this reason, *Ocydromia glabricula* and other members of this fly family are known as "dance flies."

Dance flies live all over the world and regularly swarm like this. Often, these mating swarms form near specific landmarks, such as near a tree or on a particular hillside.

LENGTH: .16 in.

DIET: Nectar

FOUND IN: Throughout Europe

LONG-TAILED DANCE FLY

(*Rhamphomyia longicauda*)

The female long-tailed dance fly prepares to attract a male by pumping up her abdomen and showing off her hairy legs. She is trying to trick a nearby male into thinking she is full of eggs and therefore grab his attention. This is a clever tactic for the hungry female because males bring with them a gift before mating, a tasty dead insect. By tricking the male into approaching her, and getting his delicious gift, the female has found a way to get a free meal.

LENGTH: .24–.4 in.

DIET: Small insects

FOUND IN: Wet woodlands throughout isolated parts of North America

GREEN LONG-LEGGED FLY

(Austrosciapus connexus)

The green long-legged fly perches on a leaf. With large and sensitive eyes, it scans the nearby bushes and trees for its prey, tiny aphids. Unlike most insects, male and female green long-legged flies depend mostly on vision to find one another. The species uses its shiny exoskeleton and flaglike wings to draw attention to itself.

The long-legged flies make up one of the largest groups of flies. In total, scientists have described 7,000 species.

LENGTH: Approximately .2 in.

DIET: Aphids and other small soft-bodied insects

FOUND IN: Throughout Australia and some neighboring islands

SEPEDON SPINIPES

Known from waterlogged rice fields in Asia, this species of so-called snail-killing fly lays its eggs on snails. Its maggots feed on the snail throughout the larval stage before pupating into an adult form which feeds upon nectar.

The snail-killing fly was released in the islands of Hawai'i 50 years ago to control the spread of human diseases carried by snails. Sadly, their successful colonization has seen some native species of snail become threatened with extinction.

LENGTH: .31 in.

DIET: Nectar

FOUND IN: Throughout wetlands of Asia

FLIES OF SMALL SIZE (DIPTERA)

On these pages we discover some of the families of fly in which species are incredibly tiny and easy to overlook. Each is a single representative of its large family grouping—the fruit flies, the drain flies, the fungus gnats, and the scuttle flies.

COMMON FRUIT FLY
(Drosophila melanogaster)

What the fruit fly lacks in size, it makes up for in personality. When landing on rotten fruits, these flies regularly flick their wings at one another to produce a noisy hum which signals their anger. They also produce special scents that tell others to back away. If this fails, pushing and shoving between fruit flies can break out.

Because this species is easy to keep in captivity, the fruit fly is a go-to study animal for scientists eager to understand how animals work. As such, it has become the insect species scientists know most about.

LENGTH: Approximately .1 in.

FOUND IN: Throughout the world

DIET: Rotting fruits and decaying vegetables

BATHROOM MOTH MIDGE
(Clogmia albipunctata)

The bathroom moth midge is neither a moth nor a midge, but a so-called drain fly—one of 2,600 species of drain fly known to scientists. Its common name comes from its furry wings, hairy body, and unusually ridged antennae that are very mothlike.

The bathroom moth midge is often found in bathrooms because its wormlike larvae feed upon the waste found in drains and plugholes. This human-made habitat resembles the tree-trunk puddles that this species seeks in the wild.

LENGTH: .12–.2 in.

FOUND IN: Tropical and temperate areas worldwide

DIET: Adults do not feed

FUNGUS GNAT
(Excechia nugatoria)

As the cold icy winds come in, *Excechia nugatoria* prepares itself for something spectacular. To survive freezing temperatures, most insects either stop their body from freezing using special chemicals or flush the water from their bodies and allow themselves to freeze. *Excechia nugatoria* does both. It uses antifreeze to stop its brain from freezing and allows its abdomen to freeze solid.

Of thousands of known species of fungus gnat, *Excechia nugatoria* is by far the toughest. In fact, it is the only known insect to survive winter through such an adaptation.

LENGTH: Approximately .08 in.

FOUND IN: Arctic regions of North America

DIET: Nectar

EURYPLATEA NANAKNIHALI

Little more than the size of a speck of dust, *Euryplatea nanaknihali* is the world's smallest fly. Even though it is almost impossible to see with the naked eye, the species possesses all of the same features as any other fly. Scientists suspect that the species lays its eggs in the head regions of ants. The larvae eat the ant's brains before pupating into adult form.

Euryplatea nanaknihali belongs to a group of flies known as scuttle flies because of their habit of running across surfaces rather than using their wings.

LENGTH: Less than .01 in.

FOUND IN: Known from a number of national parks in Thailand

DIET: Adult diet unknown

FLIES OF LIFE (DIPTERA)

Some of the world's most successful fly species are the flies that lay eggs upon dead or dying animals that hatch into flesh-eating maggots. Though maggots fill many humans with disgust, they do a vital job in cleaning away dead organisms.

HOUSEFLY
(Musca domestica)

As humans have prospered, so too has the housefly. Today, this fly species thrives in kitchens and warehouses all over the world, feasting on thrown-away items of food. One of the secrets of the housefly's success is its ability to live in both warm and cold buildings, including near the North Pole. The other reason that has contributed to its success is the female's impressive egg-laying skills. In a matter of weeks, a single female housefly can lay up to 500 eggs.

LENGTH: .24–.28 in.

FOUND IN: Near humans all over the world

DIET: Unattended kitchen waste

AFRICAN FLESH FLY
(Sarcophaga [Bercaea] africa)

The African flesh fly is not in the least bit fussy. As well as feasting upon living or dead animals, including snails, insects, and birds, its maggots are also able to digest rotting vegetables and animal droppings.

Where most female flies lay their eggs and move away, the African flesh fly carries its eggs for as long as possible, dropping them to the ground as tiny maggots at the exact moment that they hatch. This protects their eggs from being attacked by hungry wasps and their grubs.

LENGTH: Approximately .4 in.

FOUND IN: Across all continents except Antarctica

DIET: Most organic matter

COMMON GREEN BOTTLE FLY

(Lucilia sericata)

With large red eyes and a bright metallic-green abdomen, the beauty of the common green bottle fly is undeniable. Yet looks can be deceiving. The green bottle fly is another fly species that makes its living trailing humans and, particularly, farm animals. As well as laying its eggs on dead animals, this fly species also lays eggs on cuts and wounds upon the bodies of large mammals. Sheep can often fall victim to large-scale attacks from their maggots, a phenomenon known as "fly-strike."

The fact that the common green bottle fly regularly moves between dead and living animals makes it capable of spreading nasty diseases. For this reason, the common green bottle is often considered a pest. However, this beautiful fly can have its uses. For instance, its maggots can be used in hospitals to help clean wounds of nasty bacteria—a medical practice called maggot therapy.

LENGTH: .4–.55 in.

DIET: Mostly nectar

FOUND IN: Common throughout the world

FANTASTIC FLIES (DIPTERA)

Did you know that one in every ten animal species named by scientists is a fly? Not only do flies rival other insects in their ingenuity and adaptability, they also give other animals a run for their money. On these pages, we highlight four incredibly well-adapted and incredible fly species.

MYDAS FLY

(Gauromydas heros)

Almost as long as a human hand, *Gauromydas heros* may be as large as a fly can evolve to be. Yet, for all its size, this is a secretive fly that scientists know very little about.

The large size of *Gauromydas heros* may be to help it to mimic venomous wasps and hornets. Little is known about its larval stage. Scientists suspect that its larvae may live within the nests of leafcutter ants, perhaps feeding upon the beetles that live off their waste.

LENGTH: 2.75 in.

DIET: Unknown

FOUND IN: Remote parts of Brazil, Bolivia, and Paraguay

MALAYSIAN STALK-EYED FLY

(Teleopsis dalmanni)

When it first hatches as an adult from its pupa, the Malaysian stalk-eyed fly does something incredible. It pumps air into its head and forces its eyes out on extended stalks. These eyestalks are very important for males of this species, because females find the longest stalks most attractive.

As with deer stags, males often compete with one another for the interests of females. They battle by facing one another and working out which has the longest eyestalks. The fly with the littlest stalks often walks away the loser.

LENGTH: Approximately .2 in.; eyespan .2–.3 in.

DIET: Decaying vegetation and fungus

FOUND IN: Near streams and rivers throughout Southeast Asia

BAT FLY
(Basilia nana)

Like a vampire, this unusual fly seeks out and drinks blood. Yet it is not interested in human blood—it prefers the blood of bats. Unusually for a fly, the bat fly has totally lost its wings and eyes over many thousands of years. Its legs have evolved to fold backward, meaning that it moves like a spider. This allows it to grip on extra tight.

Including *Basilia nana*, there are 274 known species of bat fly and almost every species lives upon its own specific species of bat.

LENGTH: .08–1.2 in.

DIET: Bat blood

FOUND IN: The bodies of Bechstein's bats

NEW ZEALAND GLOWWORM
(Arachnocampa luminosa)

Each year, thousands of tourists travel deep into New Zealand's spectacular caves to gaze at a starry glow created by thousands of tiny bioluminescent larvae that dangle from the cave ceiling. These are the larvae of a special type of fungus gnat that lives nowhere else on Earth.

By glowing a ghostly green, the larva of *Arachnocampa luminosa* attracts tiny flies, which it captures in nets made of dripping slime. Once captured, the wormlike larva wriggles over to begin digesting its meal.

LENGTH: Larvae up to 1.6 in.

DIET: Small flies

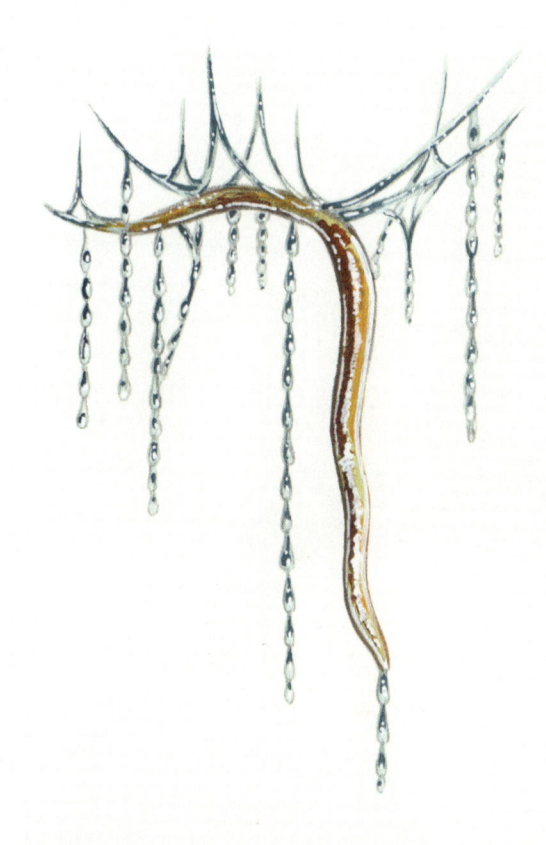

FOUND IN: Widespread in wetland caves throughout New Zealand

JUMPING BRISTLETAILS (ARCHAEOGNATHA), FIREBRATS, AND SILVERFISH (ZYGENTOMA)

For many years, the invertebrates on these pages were considered to be unrelated to the insects that live in the modern day. However, recent scientific investigations have revealed that they are, in fact, primitive insects. Fossils of these species have been discovered in Carboniferous rocks that are more than 300 million years old.

JUMPING BRISTLETAIL
(Lepismachilis y-signata)

Lepismachilis y-signata is one of 500 species known as jumping bristletails. These insects get their name from their ability to launch themselves more than a foot into the air by flexing a powerful tail. Once landed, they scurry into nearby cracks to escape being eaten.

Unlike other insects, the jumping bristletail's sense of smell is poor and its mouthparts are not very strong. It uses these mouthparts to scrape up and chew algae and other soft foods.

The bristles in its name are found on the underside of its body. Scientists think they may once have been extra legs that, over millions of years, have reduced in size.

LENGTH: .2–.4 in.

DIET: Algae, fungi, and decaying vegetation

FOUND IN: Throughout Europe and across the world

FIREBRAT
(Thermobia domestica)

The firebrat get its name from its habit of finding warm and dry places to hide, including near fires. In buildings that remain hot all year around, such as in bakeries or cafeterias, the firebrat devours leftover sugary foods and breeds quickly. A single female can lay 6,000 eggs in her lifetime. This means that, in some cases, this primitive insect can become a pest.

To digest its sugary diet, the firebrat has special bacteria in its body to break down and release energy from its meal.

LENGTH: Approximately .47 in.

DIET: Sugary materials

FOUND IN: Near human habitations across the world

SILVERFISH
(Lepisma saccharina)

The silverfish is a survivor from an age long before dinosaurs walked the Earth. In fact, fossils of invertebrate footprints suggest that its close relatives may have been among the first organisms to move onto the land more than 400 million years ago.

Silverfish walk or run along surfaces in a wiggling manner. This, combined with their shiny scales, is what gives them their common name. Unlike nearly all other insects, silverfish lack wings and their eyes are very simple—the silverfish is a creature of the night.

For millions of years, the silverfish was a cave-dweller that searched for rotting vegetation to eat. In the modern day, the silverfish has found a different kind of cave to occupy—our houses. Today, silverfish are known to eat a number of household objects including carpets, coffee, paper, photos, and sugar. Silverfish have even been seen eating their own skin after it has been shed.

LENGTH: Up to .79 in.

DIET: Sugars from a variety of household materials

FOUND IN: Houses and other buildings

NET-WINGED INSECTS (NEUROPTERA) AND SNAKEFLIES (RAPHIDIOPTERA)

For most of the age of the dinosaurs, the sky was not full of bees and butterflies, but more primitive flying insects. Some of these species have survived into the modern day. They are known as the net-winged insects (the neuropterans) and the snakeflies (the raphidiopterans). Scientists sometimes refer to these groups as the "butterflies of the Jurassic."

GREEN LACEWING
(Chrysopa perla)

To find aphids to eat, the green lacewing takes to the sky upon long wings. At the base of each wing is a simple eardrum that it uses to listen for bats. If the green lacewing hears the telltale sound of a bat approaching, it pulls its wings together and drops to the floor for safety.

The green lacewing also uses sound during the breeding season, when it generates a simple song by vibrating its body against twigs and leaves. There are approximately 2,000 species of lacewing worldwide and each species has its own unique song.

LENGTH: .4–.5 in.

DIET: Aphids

FOUND IN: Woodlands and grasslands throughout Europe and Asia

MACARONIUS OWLFLY
(Libelloides macaronius)

The Macaronius owlfly is a deadly aerial hunter. Unlike most owlflies, it searches for prey during the day and scans the sky with wraparound compound eyes that can spot prey from many directions at once.

Even the larva of the Macaronius owlfly is deadly. It camouflages itself by dressing in sand and soil grains, and waits like a crocodile with its jaws open for prey to accidentally step too close.

Its long antennae are used to sense for special chemicals in the air given off by other owlflies during the mating season.

LENGTH: Approximately .79 in.

FOUND IN: Throughout Europe

DIET: Insects

MANTIDFLY
(Dicromantispa interrupta)

There is no escaping the pair of imposing clawlike legs that this species uses as a weapon to catch its prey. Within seconds of capture, *Dicromantispa interrupta* begins to pull apart its meal using impressive mouthparts.

The resemblance to the raptorlike forelegs of the mantis gives this species and its close relatives the common name of "mantisflies" or "mantidflies." Though the two insect groups are not closely related, they have hit upon the same adaptation to catch their prey—scientists call this phenomenon "convergent evolution."

LENGTH: .79–1.2 in.

FOUND IN: Throughout Central and North America

DIET: Insects and spiders

SNAKEFLY
(Puncha ratzeburgi)

Each morning, *Puncha ratzeburgi* is on the lookout for other insects attempting to move in on its territory. These competitors may seek to steal its food source of aphids and mites, so *Puncha ratzeburgi* must be ready to defend itself. It scans the nearby leaves, its periscopelike head held high.

The unusually elongated head is what gives this species and its close relatives the common name, snakefly. Snakeflies are another prehistoric part of the insect family. Fossils of snakeflies have been found in rocks from the Jurassic period, 150 million years ago.

LENGTH: 1.6 in.

FOUND IN: Central and Eastern Europe, including upon hills and small mountains

DIET: Insects and spiders

SCORPIONFLIES (MECOPTERA) AND GLADIATORS (NOTOPTERA)

Many insects show complicated behaviors that rival those of bigger animals such as birds and reptiles. This is especially true when it comes to insect love lives. On these pages, we consider the love lives of two smaller insect groups, the scorpionflies and the so-called gladiators.

COMMON SCORPIONFLY
(Panorpa communis)

The common scorpionfly has long beaklike mouthparts that are used for pulling apart dead insects. This beak can also be used to pluck dead insects from spiderwebs without the spider knowing. Like other scorpionflies, this species is often found walking through undergrowth rather than flying.

Though it looks like a poisonous stinger, the tip of the tail of the common scorpionfly is more like a grappling hook. This adaptation is used by males to hold onto females during the breeding season.

LENGTH: 1.2 in.

DIET: Dead insects

FOUND IN: Hedgerows and patches of nettles throughout Europe and northern Asia

BLACK-TIPPED HANGINGFLY
(Hylobittacus apicalis)

The hooked tips upon the legs of the black-tipped hangingfly help it to dangle from leaves and twigs while resting. So adapted is the black-tipped hangingfly to this treetop way of life that it can no longer walk around like other insects.

To entice a female during the breeding season, the male of this species flies around with a special parcel of food that it dangles beneath its body. To better get her attention, the male sprays a special love potion onto its gift, which a female can detect within 50 ft.

LENGTH: Approximately .8 in.

FOUND IN: Isolated parts of Mexico and the US

DIET: Insects

TASMANIAN SNOW SCORPIONFLY

(Apteropanorpa tasmanica)

In spring, the Tasmanian snow scorpionfly makes an epic journey through the snow. It is searching for patches of moss that have been exposed, where it can meet and lay eggs with others of its species. And, lacking wings, it has to walk.

Scientists do not yet know what may have led to this scorpionfly becoming wingless. In all, four wingless species from this group are known, all from the far south of Australia.

LENGTH: .12–.16 in.

FOUND IN: Snow fields of Tasmania

DIET: Insects

GLADIATOR

(Tyrannophasma gladiator)

To advertise its whereabouts to others during the breeding season, *Tyrannophasma gladiator* pushes its body to the ground and vibrates, creating a wave of energy that moves through the floor. If a nearby individual feels these vibrations, it homes in so that egg-laying can begin.

For many years, scientists did not know exactly where the so-called gladiators fit into the insect family tree. Some scientists argued they may be closely related to stick insects or praying mantises. For now, they are considered as a unique family group called the Mantophasmatidae.

LENGTH: Approximately 1.26 in.

FOUND IN: The mountains of Namibia

DIET: Insects

ANGEL INSECTS (ZORAPTERA) AND WEBSPINNERS (EMBIOPTERA)

Some insect groups are found throughout the world, but are rarely spotted or recognized due to their small size. The angel insects live within rotting wood, often forming colonies within which they live protected. Webspinners are also social. Insects of this group makes special shelters from silk, under which they feed in safety.

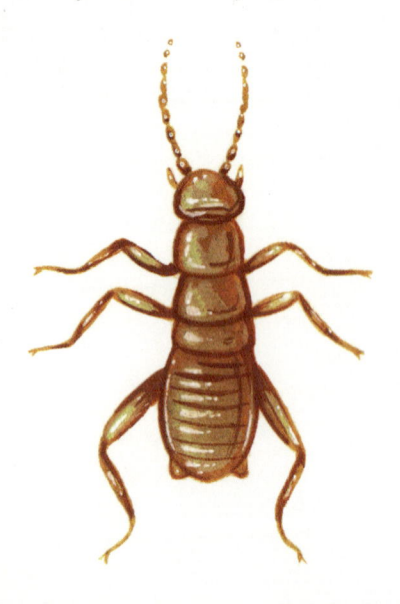

HUBBARD'S ANGEL INSECT
(Zorotypus hubbardi)

Upon being discovered by a predator, an entire colony of Hubbard's angel insects scurry and sprint toward the darkest regions of their nest. Here, the colony-mates remain until the threat moves away.

Like other angel insects, this species eats the fungi that grow upon rotting trees. When fungi is abundant, angel insects reproduce quickly. Female angel insects are able to produce clones of themselves in a process called parthenogenesis, like aphids do. When food becomes harder to find, she produces a batch of offspring with wings that go off to find better places to feed.

LENGTH: .12 in.

FOUND IN: Throughout the Americas

DIET: Fungi

ZOROTYPUS ASYMMETRISTERNUM

Discovered in 2018, *Zorotypus asymmetristernum* is only the sixth species of angel insect known from Africa. Like a mole, this angel insect species has incredibly tiny eyes. Each is little more than the size of a pinhead. These simple eyes allow *Zorotypus asymmetristernum* to detect light and dark, meaning it can find places to hide if discovered by predators.

Angel insects are perhaps the least explored of all insects. There are likely to be many more new species of angel insect discovered in the years to come.

LENGTH: .12 in.

FOUND IN: Kakamega rainforest of Kenya

DIET: Likely to eat fungi

SAUNDERS' EMBIID
(Oligotoma saundersii)

To make a safe place in which to feed, the Saunders' embiid searches for a crack in the bark of a tree and sets to work. By squirting silk from 100 or more special glands in her legs, she makes a network of silken tunnels. These are her feeding galleries, where she will chew in peace upon dead leaves, fungi, and algae.

When the time is right, she will produce a nest of eggs that she will guard from enemies such as parasitic wasps.

LENGTH: Approximately .24 in.

DIET: Plants, algae, and fungi

FOUND IN: Southern Asia; accidentally introduced into North America

APOSTHONIA MERDELYNAE

This webspinner was discovered in 2018 by intrepid researchers exploring a dormant volcano on the island of Luzon in the Philippines. It is named after a local scientist who is celebrated for training and inspiring many generations of young insect scientists.

As with all webspinners, *Aposthonia merdelynae* is very sociable. Females look after their young, often sharing their feeding galleries with family members. Together, these groups tend to the silken gallery, keeping it in good enough condition to stop predators breaking in.

LENGTH: Approximately .6 in.

DIET: Likely to include fungi

FOUND IN: The foothills of Mount Makiling in the Philippines

FLEAS (SIPHONAPTERA)

Although easy to miss, fleas are another insect group that brims with diversity. In total, the group (which scientists call Siphonaptera) contains approximately 2,500 species. Each flea species feeds exclusively on the blood of mammals or birds. By accidentally spreading diseases, fleas include among their ranks some of the most deadly insects on Earth.

ORIENTAL RAT FLEA
(Xenopsylla cheopis)

To find a blood meal, the oriental rat flea smells for the breath of its potential victims. It is highly sensitive to the carbon dioxide that animals produce as they exhale. Though it cannot fly, the oriental rat flea's impressive forelegs allow it to jump from host to host. Its hind pair of legs are capable of tensing with incredible speed and power. Jumps of 7 in. high are not uncommon for this species. These impressive leaps make it, for its size, one of the highest jumpers in the animal kingdom.

The oriental rat flea has killed more people than perhaps any other single insect species. This is because, when it bites, it injects saliva into the skin that can contain diseases. Though this species often feeds upon the blood of rats, it regularly moves between mammals, including humans. The so-called Black Death of 1347 was carried by the oriental rat flea. The disease outbreak led to the death of one in three Europeans at the time.

LENGTH: .1 in.

DIET: Mammal blood

FOUND IN: Isolated parts of all the world's continents except Antarctica

CHIGOE FLEA
(Tunga penetrans)

The female chigoe flea sees very little of the world. She drills into the outer layers of skin on her victim's body and leaves only the tip of her abdomen exposed to the air so that she can breathe. In this special hiding place safely within the skin of her host, she feeds on blood while brooding eggs. When the eggs are ready, she begins to squirt them out of the host's body onto the floor, where they hatch into tiny free-living larvae.

At less than .04 in. in length, this is the world's smallest flea species.

LENGTH: .04 in.

DIET: Blood

FOUND IN: Central and South America; also introduced to sub-Saharan Africa

BLACK AND RED FREE-TAILED BAT FLEA
(Araeopsylla goodmani)

While bats dart and whistle through the night sky, many of them carry hitchhikers in the form of bat fleas, a group that contains many different flea species.

Bat caves provide the flea's nursery grounds. Here they live as larvae before pupating into their adult form. To get the cave ceiling where the bats sleep, the newly pupated bat fleas of some species hitch a lift on earwigs.

The black and red free-tailed bat flea is among the most recently discovered of flea species. It was discovered by scientists in 2016.

LENGTH: .08 in.

DIET: Bat blood

FOUND IN: Fianarantsoa Province, Madagascar

AM I AN INSECT?

Run your fingers down the back of your neck. You'll feel lots of knobbly bones (called vertebrae) that are linked together to make your backbone. About one in twenty (5%) of the animals on Earth have this kind of skeleton. They are called the vertebrates. Vertebrate animals include frogs, newts, snakes, lizards, turtles, crocodiles, eagles, sparrows, mice, monkeys, and humans. The other 95% of animals on this planet have no obvious bones at all inside their body. They are called the invertebrates.

All insects are invertebrates. They have a tough exoskeleton, six jointed legs, and three parts (or segments) to their body: the head, thorax, and abdomen. However, there are many invertebrates that look like insects, but which—on closer inspection—are not.

In this section, we explore some of the other groups of invertebrates that are regularly mistaken for insects.

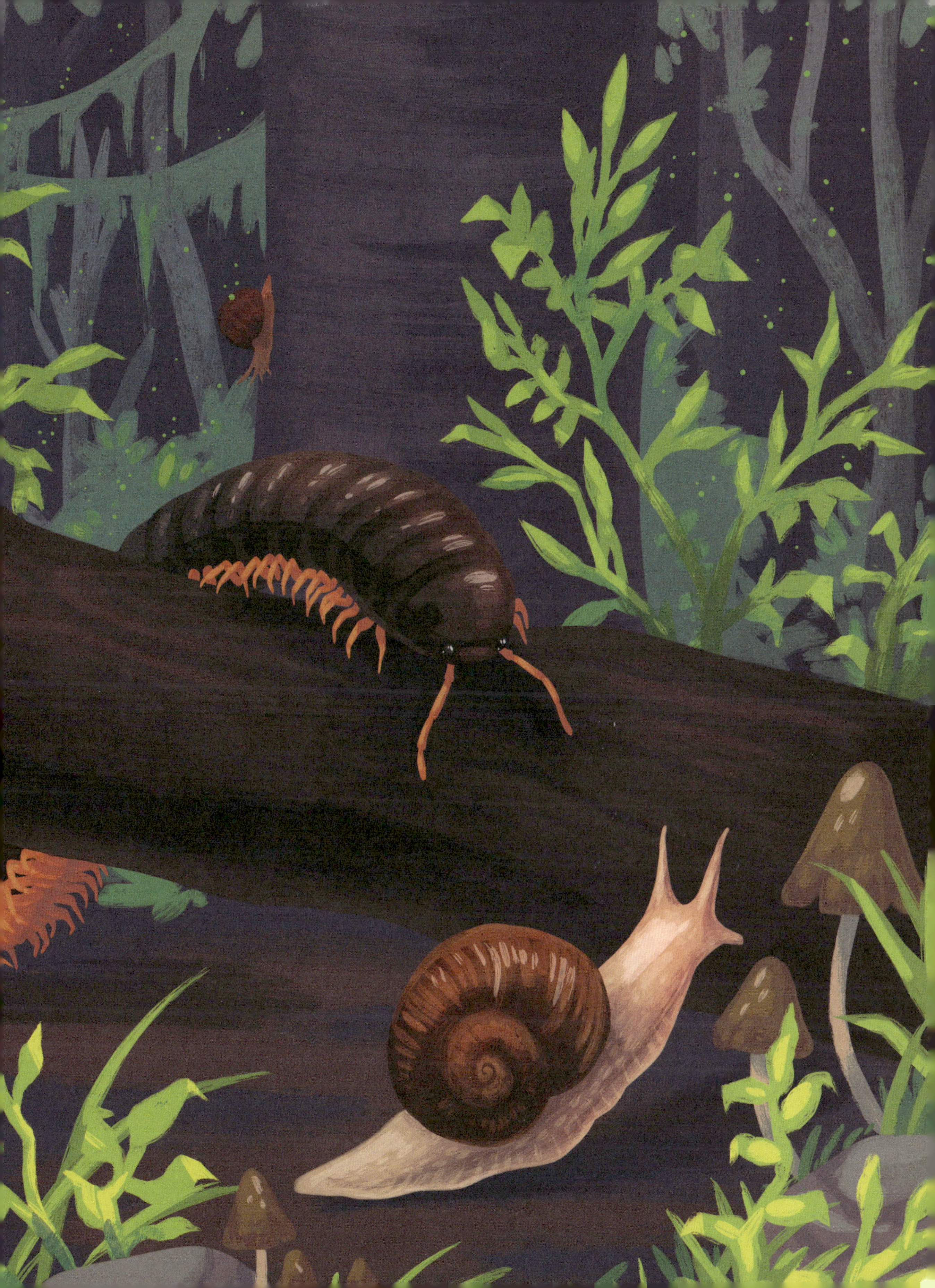

CENTIPEDES AND MILLIPEDES

Centipedes and millipedes are known for having lots and lots of legs, not just six legs like insects. In total, scientists have described 16,000 species.

Most millipedes have many more legs than centipedes—up to 750 in total. This is because millipedes use their numerous legs to push the body through the soil like a giant battering ram. Centipedes, on the whole, have fewer legs. This helps them move more quickly through the undergrowth as they search for other invertebrates to capture and eat.

Centipedes and millipedes are even more ancient than insects. They were among the very first animals to leave the sea to colonize the land more than 450 million years ago.

To work out if you are looking at a millipede or a centipede, look carefully at the body segments. If there are two pairs of legs for each segment, you are looking at a millipede. If there is a single pair of legs on each segment, you are looking at a centipede.

The **GIANT AFRICAN MILLIPEDE** is one of the world's largest land invertebrates. It protects itself from attackers by coiling into a tight spiral shape, hiding its legs so that only its hard armor is exposed. If predators continue their attack, the giant African millipede has a back-up plan: its squeezes out toxic juices that predators find disgusting.

The **SIERRA LUMINOUS MILLIPEDE** is one of only a few millipedes known to glow in the dark. These millipedes are able to produce an extremely deadly poison known as cyanide. The millipede's bioluminescence helps it to warn away predators that share its gloomy cave habitat.

The largest centipede is the **AMAZONIAN GIANT CENTIPEDE**, which can grow to almost a foot in length. This active predator hunts amphibians, small reptiles, and even small rodents. By dangling down from the ceilings of caves, it is even known to kill and eat cave-dwelling bats. Unlike venomous insects, centipedes deliver their venom with a pair of special front legs called forcipules. This venom slows the prey down and stops it from escaping.

Some centipedes hunt in extraordinary places such as in caves or on the tops of mountains. The recently discovered **WATERFALL CENTIPEDE** is even able to dive into rivers and streams to hunt water-dwelling insects. It is the first described amphibious centipede.

Sierra luminous millipede

Giant African millipede

Waterfall centipede

Amazonian giant centipede

HOW ARE CENTIPEDES AND MILLIPEDES DIFFERENT FROM INSECTS?

- Centipedes and millipedes do not have wings.
- Centipedes and millipedes have many more legs than just six.
- Centipedes and millipedes do not have a larval stage as seen in most insects.

SPIDERS AND SPIDERLIKE INVERTEBRATES

Most spiders make their living by hunting insects, which they do with great skill. Scientists think that, each year, all of the world's spiders may eat more than 800 million tonnes of insects. All spider species are adaptable, highly sensitive to their surroundings, and venomous—though thankfully, few species can bite humans. Spiders differ from insects in having four pairs of legs rather than three.

Many species hunt by producing silk from special glands near their bottom. The silk can be used for making webs to catch prey or to make silken nursery grounds in which their babies can live in safety.

Spiders are not the only eight-legged invertebrates. They are part of a large family of eight-legged invertebrates called arachnids. Other arachnids include scorpions, mites, and the secretive long-legged spiderlike organisms known as harvestmen. These are cousins of spiders.

The largest spider is the **GOLIATH BIRDEATER**, which weighs almost as much as a hamster. Though its diet is mostly made up of insects, it regularly takes on larger animals such as frogs and small snakes. To defend itself, the Goliath birdeater is able to flick into the air a cloud of tiny irritating hairs that predators do not like.

Some spiders are very colorful and make lots of effort to impress others of their species. The most celebrated is the **PEACOCK JUMPING SPIDER**, which pumps up its vibrantly colored abdomen and dances energetically while waving a single pair of legs around like tiny flags. This activity helps it get noticed during the breeding season.

The **ARABIAN FAT-TAILED SCORPION** is one of the deadliest scorpions known to humans. As with all scorpions, its sting comes from a venomous barb on its tail, which is used to immobilize prey. Scorpions also possess greatly enlarged appendages called pedipalps—otherwise known as pincers.

With a 13 in. legspan, the giant cave-living **LAOTIAN HARVESTMAN** is one of the largest of the world's harvestman species. Harvestmen differ from spiders in having a single fused body that lacks an obvious head or abdomen. Their eyes are found on the top, rather than on the front, of their bodies.

Peacock jumping spider

Laotian harvestman

Arabian fat-tailed scorpion

Goliath birdeater

HOW ARE SPIDERS AND OTHER ARACHNIDS DIFFERENT FROM INSECTS?

- Spiders and other arachnids do not have wings.
- Arachnids do not have a three-part body like an insect that contains head, thorax, and abdomen. Spiders, for instance, have a two-part body instead. They have a cephalothorax (a head) and an abdomen.
- Spiders and other arachnids do not have a larval stage—their eggs hatch into miniature versions of adults.
- Most insects do not produce silk whereas many arachnids (particularly spiders) do.

WOODLICE

Woodlice are part of a group of invertebrates called crustaceans. Like the insects, the crustaceans are an enormous group of invertebrates that thrive in lots of places, especially in the world's oceans. Like insects, crustaceans have a tough exoskeleton that they have to shed (or molt) as they grow. The legs of crustaceans, however, often split into two parts like twigs on the branch of a tree. This makes them different to insect legs.

The crustacean group has within it well-known water-dwelling animals such as crabs, lobsters, shrimps, prawns, and barnacles. Yet one secretive group of crustaceans has come from the sea and, over many millions of years, invaded the land. These are called woodlice.

Woodlice have seven pairs of jointed legs and a hard, armorlike shell which, in some species, can be rolled into a defensive ball. They carry their eggs in a special pocket called the marsupium and produce tiny babies that look like miniature versions of adults. There may be as many as 7,000 species woodlouse species worldwide.

Where most woodlice live in dark and damp environments, some woodlice have colonized drier regions. The **DESERT WOODLOUSE** walks upon stiltlike legs that keep its body away from the burning sand. It gets all of its water from the plants that it eats.

PILL BUGS are woodlice that are able to roll their armored bodies into a protective ball like an armadillo. Pill bugs rely on this behavior if they are attacked by birds or spiders. Rolling up may also help them hold onto precious water, stopping themselves from drying out.

Found in Europe and now an invader of North America, the **COMMON STRIPED WOODLOUSE** is one of the world's most common woodlice. Like many other woodlice, this species helps break down the leaf litter on the forest floor, adding nutrients to soil that help plants grow.

Some woodlice have returned to their crustacean roots and become seaside scavengers. These include the so-called **SEA SLATERS**. Sea slaters are common on rocky beaches on both sides of the Atlantic Ocean. They hide within cracks and beneath stones in rockpools.

Common striped woodlouse

Desert woodlouse

Pill bugs

Sea slater

HOW ARE WOODLICE DIFFERENT FROM INSECTS?

• Woodlice have seven pairs of legs. Insects have just three.
• Woodlice do not possess wings.
• Unlike most insects, woodlice babies resemble miniature versions of adults. Though most crustaceans do have a larval stage, this is not obvious in woodlice.
• Unlike insects, woodlice breathe using pocketed gills that resemble lungs. Insects, on the other hand, breathe by pulling air in and out of tiny holes (called spiracles) that run the length of the body.

SNAILS AND SLUGS

Snails and slugs belong to a group of animals known as mollusks. Mollusks are known for having a hard structure within their body called the mantle, a lunglike bag used for breathing and, in many cases, a rasping sandpaperlike tongue. Other mollusks include clams, limpets, squid, and octopus.

Of the 85,000 species of mollusk scientists have so far described, snails and slugs (together known as gastropods) are by far the most numerous. At least 65,000 species of gastropod are known, living in habitats all over the world, from coral reefs to caves and beaches to gardens.

Gastropods come in two forms. Snails are gastropods that can pull their bodies into their shells to protect themselves when resting, whereas "slug" is the term used to describe those gastropods that cannot. Many slugs have no shell at all. This includes most of the slugs that have made homes of our gardens.

Among the world's largest snails is the **AFRICAN LAND SNAIL**, which can weigh over 2 lbs. Like many snails, if this species fails to find a mate it can produce its own babies—it can lay as many as 1,200 eggs in a single year.

Many gastropods live underwater. The sea slug known as the **SPANISH DANCER** gets its name from its particularly beautiful swimming style. This strange slug moves by undulating the tips of its body upward and downward in the water, making it look like a flamenco dancer's skirt being waved.

One of the rarest and most endangered sea snails in the world is the **SCALY-FOOT SNAIL**. This is the only animal in the world that can produce scales made of metal. The scaly-foot snail lives upon remote volcanic vents found deep under the surface of the ocean. It is threatened by mining companies eager to harvest metals from rocks nearby.

The **COMMON GARDEN SNAIL** is one of the world's most traveled snails. Once found only in Europe, this species has accidentally been introduced to many parts of North and South America, southern Africa, Australia, and New Zealand. Its voracious appetite for plants means that many gardeners consider this species a pest.

Scaly-foot snail

African land snail

Spanish dancer

Common garden snail

HOW ARE SLUGS AND SNAILS DIFFERENT FROM INSECTS?

• Snails and slugs have no legs or wings. Land-living species move upon a big slimy underside called the foot.
• Insects pull in oxygen through lots of tiny holes called spiracles. Land-living slugs and snails have a single hole (called a respiratory pore) through which air is pulled into the body.
• Unlike insects, snails and slugs do not have segmented bodies and they do not shed their skin as they grow.
• Unlike arachnids, crustaceans, and insects, the eyes of snails and slugs are not well-developed. This is partly because land-living snails and slugs are mostly nocturnal.

INDEX

A

ACANTHASPIS PETAX 44
AGGIE BRUCHID 93
ALDERFLY, COMMON 99
AMBER PHANTOM 108

ANGEL INSECT
    SEE ALSO ZOROTYPUS
    ASSYMMETRISTERNUM
    HUBBARD'S 142
ANT 8, 25, 30, 39, 44, 48, 52
    SEE ALSO TASMANIAN INCHMAN
    DRIVER 67
    ECTION ARMY 66
    GLIDING 64
    HONEYPOT 65
    LEAFCUTTER 65, 134
    PHARAOH 68
    SLAVE-MAKING 67
    THIEF 68
APHID 84, 121
    BOOGIE-WOOGIE 48
    DARK GREEN NETTLE 48
    GIANT WILLOW 49
    WHEAT 49
APOSTHONIA MERDELYNAE 143
AQUATICA LATERALIS 83
ARACHNIDS 150-151, 155
ASSASSIN BUG
    SEE ALSO ACANTHASPIS PETAX
    AUSTRALIAN COMMON 44

B

BACCHA ELONGATA 122
BACKSWIMMER, COMMON 40
BARKLOUSE, WEB-SPINNING 34
BEAUTIFUL DEMOISELLE 16
BEE 4, 6, 39, 60, 62, 65, 69, 96, 117, 138
    SEE ALSO BUMBLEBEE, HONEY BEE
    ALFALFA LEAFCUTTER 54
    DILEMMA ORCHID 55
    NEON CUCKOO 55
    WALLACE'S GIANT 54
BEETLE 4, 5, 6, 9, 11, 15, 59, 60, 63, 134
    SEE ALSO WEEVIL
    ALPINE LONGHORN 97
    ANT 88
    ARMY ANT ROVE 75
    AUSTRALIAN SUBTERRANEAN WATER 71
    BLISTER SEE SPANISH FLY
    BOMBARDIER ANT'S GUEST 73
    BRAZILIAN DIVING 71
    DEAD-NETTLE LEAF 92
    DEVIL'S COACH HORSE 74
    EASTERN HERCULES 77
    FESTIVE TIGER 73
    FLAT BARK 95
    FLEA 93
    FOUR-SPOTTED CHECKERED 89
    FRENCH GUIANA TUMBLING FLOWER 86
    GIANT AFRICAN LONGHORN 96
    GOLDEN GROUND 72
    GOLDEN STAG 78
    GOLIATH 76
    GREAT DIVING 70
    HAIRY ROVE 75
    HUHU 97
    MEALWORM 87
    MEXICAN BEAN 84
    MOTTLED TORTOISE 82
    PICTURED ROVE 74
    PLEASING FUNGUS 94
    POULTRYHOUSE PILL 79
    RED FLAT-BARK 95
    RED-LEGGED HAM 88
    SLENDER LIZARD 94
    SPOTTED HAIRY FUNGUS 87
    STAG 78
    TITAN 96
    UNICOLOROUS CLOWN 79

WHIRLIGIG 11, 70
WHITE SCARAB 77
VIOLIN 72
ELLOW-HORNED CLERID 89
BIRD-CHERRY ERMINE 104
BLACK DANCER 100
BLACK-TIPPED HANGINGFLY 140
BOOKLOUSE
    SEE BARKLOUSE, LIPOSCELIS BOSTRYCHOPHILA, LIPOSCELIS DIVINATORIUS, MESOPSOCUS UNIPUNCTATUS
BUFF-TIP 111
BUG
    KISSING 45
    THREAD-LEGGED 45
BUMBLEBEE
    BUFF-TAILED 53
    PATAGONIAN 53
BUTTERFLY 5, 6, 8, 9, 15, 63, 102, 138
    SEE ALSO AMBER PHANTOM, DARK BLUE TIGER, EUROPEAN PEACOCK, FOREST GIANT OWL, MENELAUS BLUE MORPHO, ORANGE OAKLEAF, PAINTED LADY, QUEEN ALEXANDRA'S BIRDWING
    COMMA 110
    MONARCH 114

C

CADDISFLY
    SEE ALSO BLACK DANCER, LEPTOCERUS INTERRUPTUS, LAND CADDIS
    NORTHERN CASEMAKER 100
CATERPILLAR 4, 9, 57, 63, 102, 104, 105, 106, 107, 110, 112, 114, 116
    FLANNEL MOTH 118
    GUM-LEAF SKELETONIZER 119
    HAWAIIAN CARNIVOROUS 119
    PUSS MOTH 118
CENTIPEDES 148-149
CHRYSOCHROA FULGIDISSIMA 81

CICADA	59
AUSTRALIAN GREENGROCER	442
PHARAOH	42
COCKROACH	9, 56
GERMAN	32
MADAGASCAR HISSING	32
COENOMYIA FERRUGINEA	126
COMMON YELLOW SALLY	26
COTTONY CUSHION SCALE	51
CRANEFLY, MARSH	125
CRICKET	4
SEE ALSO SPIKED MAGICIAN, WĒTĀPUNGA	
AUSTRALIAN MOLE	22
OAK BUSH	23

D

DAMSELFLY	
SEE ALSO BEAUTIFUL DEMOISELLE	
AZURE	17
GIANT HELICOPTER	16
DANCE FLY, LONG-TAILED	128
DARK BLUE TIGER	115
DARNER, COMMON GREEN	14
DOBSONFLY, EASTERN	98
DRAGONFLY	9, 10, 31, 59
SEE ALSO DARNER, COMMON GREEN AND GLOBE SKIMMER	
EMPEROR	15
SCARLET DWARF	14
DRONEFLY	123

E

EARWIG	145
COMMON	28
GIANT MURID RAT	29
LINED	28
ST HELENA GIANT	29
EUROPEAN PEACOCK	112
EURYPLATEA NANAKNIHALI	131

F

FAIRYFLY	59
FIREBRAT	136
FIREFLY	11
SEE ALSO AQUATICA LATERALIS	
GLOW WORM	29
FEMME FATALE	83
ROVER	82
FIRE GRID BURNET	102
FISHFLY	99
FLEA	
BLACK AND RED FREE-TAILED BAT	145
CHIGOE	145
ORIENTAL RAT	144
FLY	4, 6, 8, 9, 11, 30, 79, 119
SEE ALSO COENOMYIA FERRUGINEA, CRANEFLY, DANCE FLY, EURYPLATEA NANAKNIHALI, GNAT, HANGING THIEF, HORSEFLY, HOUSEFLY, HOVERFLY, HYPERALONIA MORIO, MIDGE, MOSQUITO, OCYDROMIA GLABRICULA, ROBBER FLY, SEPEDON SPINIPES	
AFRICAN FLESH	132
BAT	135
BLACK SOLDIER	126
COMMON FRUIT	130
COMMON GREEN BOTTLE	133
GREEN LONG-LEGGED	129
HIPPO	127
MALAYSIAN STALK-EYED	134
MYDAS	134
FOREST GIANT OWL	113
FROGHOPPER, MEADOW	43

G

GARDENIA BEE HAWK	117
GLADIATOR	141
GLOBE SKIMMER	10, 15
GLOW-WORM	
COMMON	82
NEW ZEALAND	11, 135
GNAT, FUNGUS	131, 135
GOLDEN BUPRESTID	80
GRASSHOPPER	8, 9, 20, 31, 93
GREEN BLADDER	19
HORSEHEAD	18
MONKEY	19
RAINBOW	18

H

HANGING THIEF	121
HAWAIIAN LEAF-MINER	105
HORNTAIL, GREATER	62
HONEY BEE	44
WESTERN	52
HORNET	107, 134
GIANT ASIAN	60
HORSEFLY, COMMON	127
HOUSEFLY	79, 132
HOVERFLY	
SEE ALSO BACCHA ELONGATA, DRONEFLY	
AMERICAN	123
DIMORPHIC BEAR	122
HUMMINGBIRD HAWKMOTH	103
HYPERALONIA MORIO	120

J

JEWEL BEETLE	
SEE CHRYSOCHROA FULGIDISSIMA, GOLDEN BUPRESTID, TEMOGNATHA ALTERNATA	
JEWEL BUG, METALLIC	47
JUMPING BRISTLETAIL	136

K

KNOBBED SALMONFLY	27

L

LACEWING	9
GREEN	138
LADYBUG	48, 89
SEE ALSO BEETLE, MEXICAN BEAN	
HARLEQUIN	85
SCALE-EATING	85
SEVEN-SPOT	84
LAND CADDIS	101
LARGE YELLOW UNDERWING	117
LEPTOCERUS INTERRUPTUS	101
LIPOSCELIS BOSTRYCHOPHILA	34
LIPOSCELIS DIVINATORIUS	35
LOCUST	11
AUSTRALIAN PLAGUE	20
DESERT	21
MIGRATORY	20
LOUSE	
BROWN BEAR	37
GOOSE BODY	37
GOPHER CHEWING	36
HEAD	36

M

MACROTERMES GILVUS	33
MANTIDFLY	139
MANTIS	8, 23, 40, 45, 80, 139, 141
ASIAN ANT	30
CHINESE	31
MEDITERRANEAN	31
WALKING FLOWER	30
MAYFLY	8, 11, 98
SEE ALSO SEPIA DUN	
GREEN DRAKE	12
STENACRON	13
TISZA	13
MEALYBUG, PINEAPPLE	51
MENELAUS BLUE MORPHO	108
MESOPSOCUS UNIPUNCTATUS	35
MIDGE	4, 98, 125
BATHROOM MOTH	130
FROG-BITING	124
PHANTOM	124
MILLIPEDE	148–149
MOSQUITO	17, 98, 125
SEE ALSO PADDLE-LEGGED BEAUTY	
MOSS BUG	
CHILEAN	50
JUMPING	50
MOTH	5, 8, 9, 11, 63, 99, 100, 110, 112, 114, 118
SEE ALSO BIRD-CHERRY ERMINE, BUFF-TIP, CATERPILLAR, FIRE GRID BURNET, GARDENIA BEE HAWK, HAWAIIAN LEAF-MINER, HUMMMINGBIRD HAWKMOTH, LARGE YELLOW UNDERWING, SILKMOTH	
ATLAS	106
COMET	113
COMMON CLOTHES	104
HANDMAIDEN	102
HORNET	107
IO	112
MORGAN'S SPHINX	116
MORNING-GLORY PLUME	105
PEPPERED	111
YUCCA	116

O

OCYDROMIA GLABRICULA	126
ORANGE OAKLEAF	110
OWLFLY, MACARONIUS	138

P

PADDLE-LEGGED BEAUTY	125
PAINTED LADY	7, 115
PARENT BUG	47

Q

QUEEN ALEXANDRA'S BIRDWING	109

R

ROBBER FLY, YELLOW FEATHERY ANTENNAE	120

S

SAUNDERS' EMBIID	143
SAWFLY	
SEE ALSO HORNTAIL, GREATER; WOODWASP	
GREEN	63
SCALE INSECT	
SEE COTTONY CUSHION SCALE; MEALYBUG, PINEAPPLE	
SCARAB	
SEE ALSO BEETLE, GOLIATH; BEETLE, EASTERN HERCULES; BEETLE, WHITE SCARAB	
SACRED	76
SCORPIONFLY	
SEE ALSO BLACK-TIPPED HANGINGFLY COMMON	140
TASMANIAN SNOW	141
SEPEDON SPINIPES	129
SEPIA DUN	12
SHIELD BUG, GIANT	46
SILKMOTH	4
DOMESTIC	107
SILVERFISH	137

SLUGS	154-155
SNAILS	72, 129, 132, 154-155
SNAKEFLY	139
SPANISH FLY	86
SPIDERS	8, 10, 15, 16, 34, 44, 45, 61, 89, 91, 100, 104, 109, 135, 140, 150-151, 152
SPIKED MAGICIAN	23
STICK INSECT	9, 18, 141
SEE ALSO WATER STICK INSECT	
DEVIL RIDER	24
GOLIATH	25
PHRYGANISTRIA CHINENSIS ZHAO	24
STONEFLY	11, 98
SEE ALSO COMMON YELLOW SALLY, KNOBBED SALMONFLY	
ALASKAN	27
OTWAY	26
STYLOPS MELITTAE	69
SYNTERMES DIRUS	33

T

TEMOGNATHA ALTERNATA	80
TERMITE	39, 54
SEE ALSO MACROTERMES GILVUS, SYNTERMES DIRUS	
THRIPS	
KLADOTHRIPS INTERMEDIUS	39
MELON	38
MIROTHRIPS ARBITER	38
THRIPS SETIPENNIS	39
TOE BITER	41
TREEHOPPER, BRAZILIAN	43
TWISTED-WINGED INSECT	
SEE STYLOPS MELITTAE, XENOS VERSPARUM	

W

WASP	8, 21, 39, 46, 52, 62, 64, 66, 84, 89, 90, 96, 107, 121, 122, 126, 132, 134, 143
SEE ALSO FAIRFLY, HORNET	
COMMON	61
EMERALD COCKROACH	56
GIANT ICHNEUMON	57
HYPER-PARASITIC ICHNEUMON	57
JUMPING GALL	58
KIKIKI FAIRY	59
MEXICAN HONEY	61
PAPER	38, 60, 69
PARASITIC FIG	58
WATER STICK INSECT	8, 40
WEBSPINNER	
SEE APOSTHONIA MERDELYNAE, SAUNDERS' EMBIID	
WEEVIL	93
ACORN	90
EUSOCIAL	91
RAFFE	90
RHIGUS	91
WĒTĀPUNGA	22
WOODLICE	152-153
WOODWASP	
PARASITIC	63
SIREX	62

X

XENOS VERSPARUM	69

Z

ZOROTYPUS ASSYMMETRISTERNUM	142

Brimming with creative inspiration, how-to projects, and useful information to enrich your everyday life, Quarto Knows is a favorite destination for those pursuing their interests and passions. Visit our site and dig deeper with our books into your area of interest: Quarto Creates, Quarto Cooks, Quarto Homes, Quarto Lives, Quarto Drives, Quarto Explores, Quarto Gifts, or Quarto Kids.

Encyclopedia of Insects © 2020 Quarto Publishing plc.
Text © 2020 Jules Howard.
Illustrations © 2020 Miranda Zimmerman.

First published in 2020 by Wide Eyed Editions, an imprint of The Quarto Group.
100 Cummings Center, Suite 265D, Beverly, MA 01915, USA.
T +1 978-282-9590 F +1 978-283-2742 www.QuartoKnows.com

The right of Jules Howard to be identified as the author of this work and Miranda Zimmerman to be identified as the illustrator of this work has been asserted by them in accordance with the Copyright, Designs and Patents Act, 1988 (UK).

All rights reserved.

No part of this publication may be reproduced, stored in a retrieval system, or transmitted, in any form, or by any means, electrical, mechanical, photocopying, recording or otherwise without the prior written permission of the publisher or a licence permitting restricted copying.

A catalogue record for this book is available from the British Library.

ISBN 978-0-7112-4915-8

The illustrations were created digitally.
Set in Bourton and Source Serif Pro.

Published by Georgia Amson-Bradshaw
Designed by Myrto Dimitrakoulia
Project edited by Katy Flint
Copy-edited by Rachel Minay
Production by Dawn Cameron
Manufactured in Guangdong, China CC032020

9 8 7 6 5 4 3 2 1

NOV 2020